De Havilland
Aircraft of World War One

Below: One of the D.H.9A squadrons working up to operational standard at the time of the Armistice was No. 155 at Chingford. It was intended to be fully equipped by 31 October 1918, and on 22 October eight of its allocated D.H.9As were at Hendon, five at Kenley and four at Norwich. One of the Hendon eight on that date was E8553, the subject of this photograph.

De Havilland

Aircraft of World War One

J. M. BRUCE

ARMS AND
ARMOUR

Arms and Armour Press
A Cassell Imprint
Villiers House, 41-47 Strand, London WC2N 5JE

Distributed in the USA by Sterling Publishing Co. Inc.,
387 Park Avenue South, New York, NY 10016-8810

Distributed in Australia by Capricorn Link (Australia) Pty. Ltd,
P.O. Box 665, Lane Cove, New South Wales 2066

British Library Cataloguing in Publication Data
Bruce, J. M. (John Mcintosh) *1923–*
De Havilland aircraft of World War One
1. Military aircraft. History
I. Title
623.746

ISBN 1-85409-069-0

Edited and designed by Roger Chesneau
Typeset by Typesetters (Birmingham) Ltd, West Midlands
Camerawork by M&E Reproductions, North Fambridge, Essex
Printed and bound in Great Britain by Courier International, Tiptree, Essex

CONTENTS

INTRODUCTION

'Ah! de Havilland!' sighs today's nostalgic, but his thoughts are, deservedly, with assorted Moths, Dragon Rapides, the exquisite little Dragonfly or, if in martial vein, possibly the peerless Mosquito or elegant Hornet. Yet there were great de Havilland aircraft during the Kaiser's war, and it was in them that their designer wrote his signature indelibly on the history of aviation.

Geoffrey de Havilland was in every sense a pioneer of aviation. Not only did he personally design and build his first biplane of 1909 but he also designed its 45hp engine. That aircraft crashed without flying, but he immediately set about producing a second design, this time building his own variation of the basic box-kite configuration exemplified by the Henry Farman Type III (photograph 1). When, late in 1910, he was engaged by His Majesty's Balloon Factory as a designer and test pilot, his aircraft

was also officially acquired. It soon received the official designation F.E.1 (Farman Experimental No.1), and Geoffrey de Havilland made phenomenal progress: in 1911 he designed the B.E.1, itself highly successful by the standards of its time; and he subsequently developed not only that aircraft but also several other Royal Aircraft Factory designs, the most notable of these being the B.S.1 (soon renamed S.E.2), a single-seat scout of outstanding performance which flew early in 1913.

He left the RAF to join G. Holt Thomas' Aircraft Manufacturing Company at Hendon in May 1914. The firm was the British licensee for the making of Farman aircraft, but Geoffrey de Havilland took up his new post with the intention of designing new and original aircraft. The advent of war so soon after his move demanded that his designs be for military aircraft – photograph 2 shows

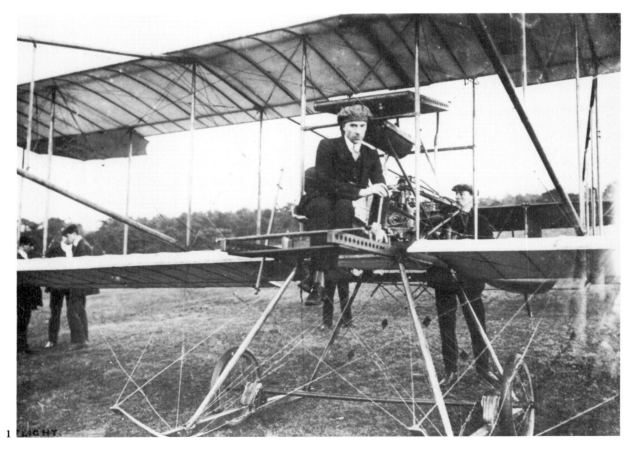

1

2

de Havilland, still flying his own designs, at Hendon in the cockpit of a D.H.9A – and these are the subject of this book.

Here the primary object has been to provide a broad, illustrated coverage of the wartime de Havilland designs, which from an early date had a significant influence on the aerial warfare of the time. Although the D.H.2 was not specifically designed to be a counter-weapon to the Fokker monoplane types, it proved to be one of the fighters that succeeded in containing this particular threat. The histories of such later types as the D.H.4, D.H.9 and D.H.9A are so long, so varied and so colourful that full-length individual monographs would be needed to do them justice. What is presented here, therefore, is confined to their wartime evolution and employment. The D.H.11, 14 and 15 are included because they owed their conception to the requirements of that war, and their designs were begun during the conflict.

Although the parent firm was the Aircraft Manufacturing Co. Ltd., its wartime products were all known by the name of their designer, a distinction and compliment that was probably unique at the time. The firm's original title was cumbersome, and shortly before 2 October 1918 it was neatly abbreviated to Airco. This may have been merely a formalization of an in-house practice, for it seems likely that the Airco name was in popular use earlier in the war. The numerical sequence of D.H. types continued uninterrupted after the formation of the de Havilland Aircraft Co. Ltd. on 25 September 1920 and lasted until the company lost its identity in December 1959, when it was absorbed into the Hawker-Siddeley Group.

The weights-and-performance table in Appendix A reflects the great number of variants that were created during the First World War. In large part they were so numerous because the period threw up substantial difficulties in aero-engine development and production. Appendix A contains a small number of blank spaces in the performance table (e.g., against the D.H.2 with Clerget engine), as do the records of bases of United States Air Service aero squadrons that, as far as is known, arrived too late to participate operationally in the war. These have been provided to enable readers who know or find these figures or facts to add them as appropriate.

Many friends have contributed in various ways to this compilation. To all who provided or lent photographs, as credited, I am grateful for their generous help; and I would add a special word of thanks to Rolly Bliss and his daughter Christy, and to Walter F. Gemeinhardt, for their great endeavours on the American side of the Atlantic. Above all, and as always, I am greatly indebted to Stuart Leslie for massive help and stalwart support; and to Bruce Robertson for his ever-ready and immensely knowledgeable help in matters factual.

Lastly, I dedicate this book, with great affection, to the memory of my friend and colleague of many years, Maurice ('Bill') Sayer, aeronautical engineer, pilot, aviation historian *par excellence* and superlative restorer of early aircraft. An enduring testimony to his outstanding talents is to be found in many of the aircraft now in the Royal Air Force Museum at Hendon: of these, perhaps the finest is the D.H.9A, the only surviving example of its type.

J. M. Bruce

DE HAVILLAND D.H.1, D.H.1A

Role: (D.H.1) Two-seat trainer; (D.H.1A) two-seat fighter-reconnaissance aircraft.
Powerplant: (D.H.1) 1 × 80hp Renault; (D.H.1A) 1 × 120hp Beardmore.
Armament: (D.H.1) None; (D.H.1A) one 0.303in Lewis machine gun.
First flight: (D.H.1) Late January 1915.*

Contractors	Contract nos.	Serial nos.	Qty. ordered	Qty. delivered	Remarks
Aircraft Mfg. Co.		4220	1	1	
Savage	{ A.3220	4600–4648	49	49	
	{ 87/A/500	A1611–A1660	50	50	

*The precise dates of first flights are known for only a few types, and dates of last flights cannot now be determined. The dates of first flights quoted throughout this book are, therefore, approximate.

The prototype D.H.1 is seen in photograph **3** soon after completion and before it was fitted with air brakes. It had been intended to fit a more powerful engine than the 70hp Renault actually installed: the original choice (so it was reported) was the 100hp Green. That was the designed power unit of the contemporary Royal Aircraft Factory F.E.2a, and it was alleged that the RAF claimed the entire output of the Green for that aircraft (though doubtless matters of contract and the production capability of the Green's makers affected the situation). Visible in this photograph are the housings, in the V-struts of the undercarriage, for the special shock absorbers that consisted of coil springs with small oleo dampers.

Soon after its emergence, the D.H.1 prototype was fitted with air brakes. These were small aerofoil-like surfaces mounted on a spanwise shaft that passed through the nacelle close behind the forward centre-section struts; they could be rotated to a position normal to the airstream. The aircraft is seen in photograph **4** at Hendon; behind it is a Deperdussin

K. M. MOLSON

3

FLIGHT

4

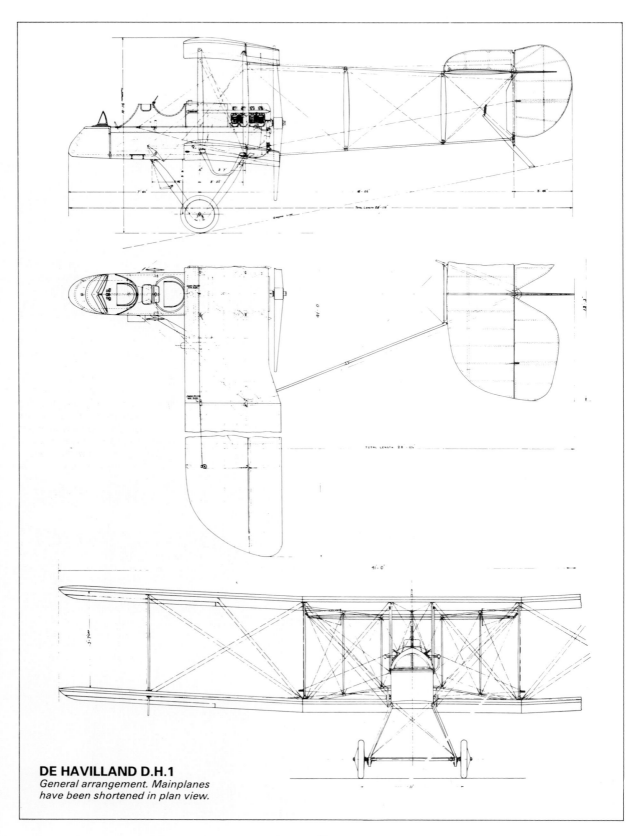

DE HAVILLAND D.H.1
*General arrangement. Mainplanes
have been shortened in plan view.*

5

monoplane of the RNAS, No.885. When the D.H.1 prototype was photographed at Farnborough, not later than 4 February 1915 (the date associated with photograph 5), its air

brakes were not present. The hole in the decking through which their shaft passed can be seen in this view of the aircraft. The high and close coaming about the observer's cockpit was

peculiar to the prototype: it would have impeded his use of any kind of gun.

The production D.H.1 had the 80hp Renault engine and, as far as is known, was used only for training purposes. Photograph **6** shows an aircraft of the first production batch (4600–4648), built by Savages Ltd. Its precise identity is unknown, but it had an early form of pressure head for the air-speed indicator on the forward inner interplane strut. The unusual forward-led exhaust pipes were a characteristic of the type.

With the installation of a 120hp Beardmore engine the type was redesignated D.H.1A, but few aircraft were so favoured. Six (4606, 4607 and 4619–4622) were sent to the Middle East and saw operational use with No. 14 Squadron RFC in Palestine. The first of these, 4606, is the subject of photograph **7**, taken at Hendon. Its batch predecessor, 4605, was flown in comparative trials with the F.E.2b No.6337 in June 1916. The D.H.1 had an appreciably better performance than the F.E.2b, proved to be more manoeuvrable and gave its observer a greater field of view and fire. The report concluded: 'Both machines are stable and easy to fly, but the de Havilland is quicker to manoeuvre and lighter on its controls.' However, the F.E.2b was already in large-scale production, and the D.H.1A remained a minor type.

6

7

D.H.1 UNITS, BASES AND MARKINGS[1]

OPERATIONAL UNITS (RFC)

Squadron	Bases	Sqn. markings
14	Kantara, Ismailia	At least one aircraft had skull and cross-bones device painted on nose of nacelle

TRAINING UNITS[2]

Central Flying School	Upavon
6 RS/TS	Catterick
8 RS/TS	Netheravon
10 RS/TS	Joyce Green
19 RS/TS	Hounslow
35 RS/TS	Filton
46 RS/TS	Bramham Moor

59 RS/TS	Yatesbury	A1638 of No. 59 RS had lower nacelle nose painted white
200 Depot Sqn.	East Retford	A1643, A1653 and A1657 of No. 200 DS had two horizontal white bands painted round nacelle nose

[1]Regrettably, it has not been possible to compile an adequate and accurate record of the markings of training units mentioned in this book. A great many of the official records relating to wartime training units were deliberately destroyed some years ago and before official files became available for general study.

[2]RFC flying training units were known as Reserve Aeroplane Squadrons until January 1916. They were then redesignated Reserve Squadrons (RS), which term lasted until 31 May 1917; thereafter they were named Training Squadrons (TS).

W. EVANS

8

Photograph **8** shows, in the heat of its unsympathetic theatre of war, one of No. 14 Squadron's D.H.1As. A combat victory was won on 2 August 1916 when one of the squadron's D.H.1As drove down an Aviatik and forced it to land near Salmana.

A closer look at the D.H.1A of No. 14 Squadron illustrated in photograph **9** reveals that there was a second mounting for a Lewis gun between the cockpits and that the observer's spare ammunition magazine were carried in external racks. Also visible, near the top of the forward centre-section strut, is a windmill-driven petrol pump. The nose of the nacelle bore a skull-and-crossbones marking.

9

DE HAVILLAND D.H.2

Role: Single-seat fighter.
Powerplant: 1 × 100hp Gnome Monosoupape, 110hp Le Rhône 9J or 110hp Clerget 9Z; (experimental) 1 × 80hp Le Rhône (5967).
Armament: One 0.303in Lewis machine gun (some D.H.2s of No. 24 Sqn. had two Lewis guns). A few aircraft (e.g. 5986, 7862) had six Le Prieur rockets, and 5961 was tested with a Maxim gun in January 1917.
First flight: 1 June 1915.

Contractors	Contract nos.	Serial nos.	Qty. ordered	Qty. delivered	Remarks
Aircraft Mfg. Co.		4732	1	1	
		5335–5383	49	–	Contract cancelled.
	87/A/36	5916–6015	100	100	Recorded as 'De Havilland (2a) Scouts'.
	87/A/386	7842–7941	100	100	
		8725	(1)	(1)	Transferred from RFC to RNAS; subsequently transferred back to RFC.
		A305	(1)	(1)	Allotted number A305 at No. 1 AD, St-Omer, on 29 October 1916. Originally had 110hp Le Rhône engine.
	87/A/386	A2533–A2632	100	100	
	87/A/386	A4764–A4813	50	50	
	87/A/728	A4988–A5087	100	100	
	87/A/728	B1389	1	(?)	Additional experimental aircraft under contract. Delivery not confirmed.

Closely following the D.H.1 came the D.H.2, a scaled-down single-seat derivative of the pusher design. Photograph **10** captures an early appearance, at Hendon, of the prototype in its initial form, when it had a small rudder without balance area. The rudder and fin of the prototype were soon enlarged, however, and the cockpit opening was modified, as seen in photograph **11**. A mounting for a movable Lewis gun was fitted on the port side.

For evaluation, the D.H.2 prototype was flown at Hendon on 22 June

10

11

12

13

14

15

1915 by Captain R. M. Pike, a Flight Commander of No. 5 Squadron RFC (photograph **12**). On acceptance by the RFC the aircraft was numbered 4732, was sent to France for operational trials and was received by No. 5 Squadron at Abeele on 26 July. No. 4732's operational career was brief. In No. 5 Squadron it was flown by Captain Pike, who fought an inconclusive combat on it on or shortly before 29 July 1915. Pike was himself shot down and killed on 9 August and 4732 fell into German hands. Although extensively damaged, the D.H.2 was rebuilt remarkably thoroughly by its captors, who not only made a new and more

rounded rudder but also carefully repainted its tricolour stripes and re-applied its serial number in Germanic style. Despite this reconstruction (see photograph **13**) it seems unlikely that 4732 was ever flown by any German pilot.

An early D.H.2 of the first production batch, 5925 (photograph **14**) was with No. 24 Squadron in March 1916, at which time it had a French-made Monosoupape engine, No. 6038.B.475. On 25 April, 2/Lt. S. E. Cowan, flying 5925, drove down a Fokker monoplane out of control near Flers; on 19 July, Lt. F. W. Honnett destroyed an enemy aircraft near Achiet; on 9 August, Captain J. O.

Andrews scored an out-of-control success south of Mory; and on 3 November, near Bapaume, a Halberstadt D.II suffered a similar fate at the hands of 2/Lt. E. C. Pashley on 5925. This D.H.2 registered three more combat successes: on 22 November 1916 2/Lt. K. Crawford shared with Captain J. O. Andrews the defeat of a German two-seater near Les Boeufs; and on the following day Lt. R. H. M. S. Saundby (the later Air Marshal Sir Robert Saundby, KCB, KBE, MC, DFC, AFC, DL) sent down an Albatros D.II out of control near Bapaume. No. 5925's last recorded victory was Lt. K. Crawford's fourth – an Albatros D.II destroyed near Gouzeaucourt on 2 April 1917. The aircraft was flown back to England on 22 May 1917 and photograph 14 shows it at Brooklands, its interplane struts still bearing traces of the broad red and white stripes favoured by No. 24 Squadron.

No. 785 was sent to France in a packing case in June 1916; photograph 15 was taken at No. 2 Aircraft Depot, Candas, and shows the aircraft with side and upper surfaces painted in P.C.10; only the fin is left in natural fabric. The size of the production-type rudder's modest balance area can be seen in this side view, and the aircraft has the four-blade propeller of type T.7928, initially the standard propeller for the F.E.8 and

D.H.2 UNITS, BASES AND MARKINGS

OPERATIONAL UNITS (RFC)

Squadron	Bases	Sqn. markings
5	Abeele	None known
11	Bertangles	None known
14	Deir el Belah	None known
18	Treizennes, Auchel, Bruay	None known
24	St-Omer, Bertangles, Chipilly, Flez	Outer interplane struts painted red and white
29	St-Omer, Abeele, Le Hameau	None known
32	Auchel, Treizennes, Vert Galant, Doullens, Léalvillers	None known
47	Yanesh, Hadzi Junas, Kalabac	None known
RFC/RNAS Composite Fighting Sqn.	Hadzi Junas	None known
111	Deir el Belah	None known
'X' Flt.	Aqaba, El Gueria	None known

SQUADRONS MOBILIZING

No. 24, Hounslow; No. 28, Gosport; No. 35, Narborough; No. 40, Gosport; No. 41, Gosport.

TRAINING UNITS

Central Flying School, Upavon; No. 6 RS/TS, Catterick; No. 10 RS/TS, Joyce Green, Shawbury; No. 13 RS/TS, Dover; No. 20 RS/TS, Wye; No. 22 RS/TS, Abu Qir.
Scout School, No. 1 Aircraft Depot, St-Omer.
No. 1 School of Aerial Fighting, Ayr.
School of Aerial Fighting, Loch Doon.
Instructional airframes to School of Military Aeronautics, Oxford (7924), and No. 8 School of Aeronautics, Cheltenham (A2600, A2632).

---

later standardized for the D.H.2. A specimen T.7928 propeller had been sent to No. 2 Aircraft Depot on 12 April 1916 with instructions that it be tested on a D.H.2. The consequence of the order is unknown, but in mid-July 1916 the Officers Commanding the 10th and 11th Wings reported that in Squadrons Nos. 32 and 29 respectively the D.H.2s were fitted with F.E.8 propellers and these were much preferred to the two-blade I.P.C.70 propeller previously used.

In No. 32 Squadron, No.7907 had a circular marking on its wheel covers, perhaps as a Flight distinction (photograph **16**). This D.H.2 was at Hendon on 20 July 1916, on which date it was allocated to the RFC in France. It was reported as being with No. 32 Squadron by 2 September 1916, but it was wrecked ten days later. The remains were sent to No. 2 Aircraft Depot, where 7907 was struck off charge on 16 September.

Also of No. 32 Squadron, No. 7862 is seen in photograph **17** with launching tubes for le Prieur rockets on its outer interplane struts: the upper surfaces of the lower wings have been protected, about the lower ends of the struts, by sheet aluminium. Another D.H.2 that was fitted with rockets was No. 5956 of No. 29 Squadron, which was tested on 30 September 1916. No. 7862 was allocated to the RFC with the Expeditionary Force on 15 June 1916, went to France in a transit case later that month, was with No. 32 Squadron by September 1916

and was still with that unit in January 1917.

RFC pilots first compared the D.H.2 with the French Nieuport 16 on 16 April 1916, about four weeks after the Corps received its first Nieuport 16, No. 5171. This Nieuport was flown by Captain M. McB. Bell-Irving, the unidentified D.H.2 by 2/Lt. J. D. Latta: the D.H.2 took 20 minutes 45 seconds to reach an altitude of 10,000 feet, the Nieuport only 11 minutes 18 seconds, and it was estimated that the Nieuport was 10–12mph faster than the D.H.2. In May 1916 the French authorities asked for a D.H.2 for comparative trials. Immediate instructions were given to 4th Brigade and No. 2 Aircraft Depot, and on 17 May Lt. D.

16

17

WG. CDR. G. H. LEWIS DFC

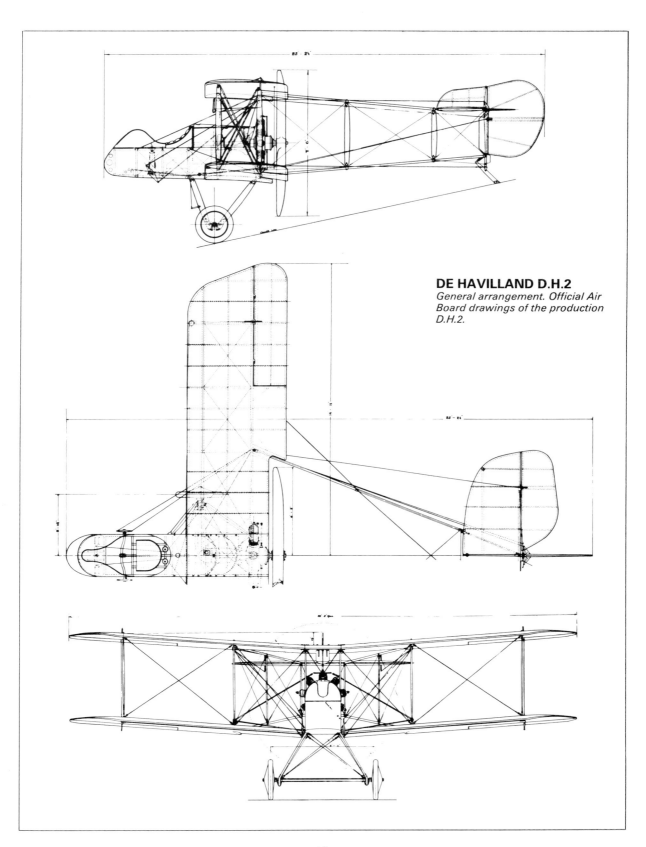

DE HAVILLAND D.H.2
General arrangement. Official Air Board drawings of the production D.H.2.

18

Wilson of No. 24 Squadron flew No. 5989 (photograph **18**) to Villacoublay. The French trials included a comparison with the Nieuport, in which the French fighter was considered to be the superior; and on 17 July 1916 the French Minister of War wrote to Captain Lord Innes-Ker of the British Aviation Supplies Depot, Paris, that the French experiments with the D.H.2 had concluded that day. Its engine had earlier been returned to the RFC but apparently it took some time to find a replacement for it was not until 21 September that Lt. N. Brearley of No. 29 Squadron flew No. 5989 back to No. 2 Aircraft Depot, Candas. The aircraft was subsequently used by No. 24 Squadron and survived its operational service to be flown back to England on 11 July 1917.

Some D.H.2s bore their serial numbers in relatively large characters on the sides of the nacelle. This may have been a specific practice of a training unit or station. It is exemplified on A4991 (photograph **19**), which at one time was used by No. 13 Reserve Squadron at Dover.

19

DE HAVILLAND D.H.3, D.H.3A

Role: Three-seat bomber.
Powerplant: (D.H.3) 2 × 120hp Beardmore; (D.H.3A) 2 × 160hp Beardmore.
Armament: (D.H.3) At least two 0.303in Lewis machine guns; bomb load.
First flight: (D.H.3) Before May 1916.

Contractors	Contract nos.	Serial nos.	Qty. ordered	Qty. delivered	Remarks
Aircraft Mfg. Co.	87/A/337	7744–7745	2	1	
	87/A/744	A5088–A5137	50	–	Contract cancelled.

The D.H.3 (photograph **20**) was a remarkably original design. As early as 25 May 1915, Geoffrey de Havilland started work on a design for a twin-engine biplane that would carry fuel for six hours within an all-up weight of 4,550lb. The engines were to be installed as pushers; although he initially thought of using 'two Austro-Daimler or similar' engines, de Havilland considered two Gnome Monosoupapes, and by 27 July 1915 had more ambitious thoughts of using two 140hp RAF 4a engines. By that time he had adopted an unusual configuration in which the lower wings were attached to the upper longerons of the fuselage; the V-struts of the undercarriage were secured to the outboard ends of the lower centre section, thus providing a wide-track structure. The D.H.3 had the particular distinction of being the first D.H. type to have the characteristically elegant form of fin and rudder that was used, with subtle variations, on many succeeding de Havilland aircraft.

With its wing span of nearly 61ft, the D.H.3 was appreciably larger than contemporary operational RFC aeroplanes and would have occupied more hangar space. Its wings were therefore designed to fold. Although no propellers were in place when photograph **21** was taken, the extension shaft of the port 120hp Beard-

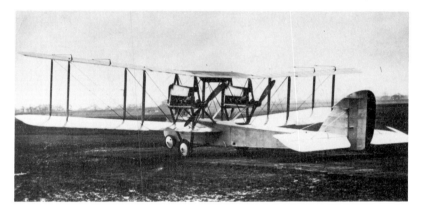

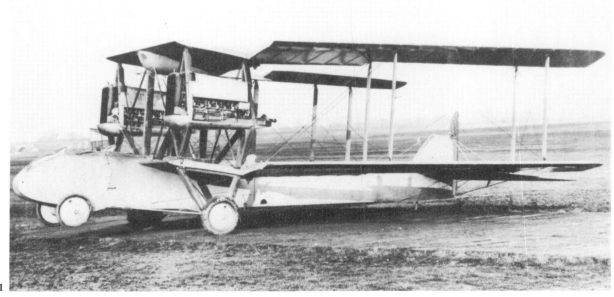

20

21

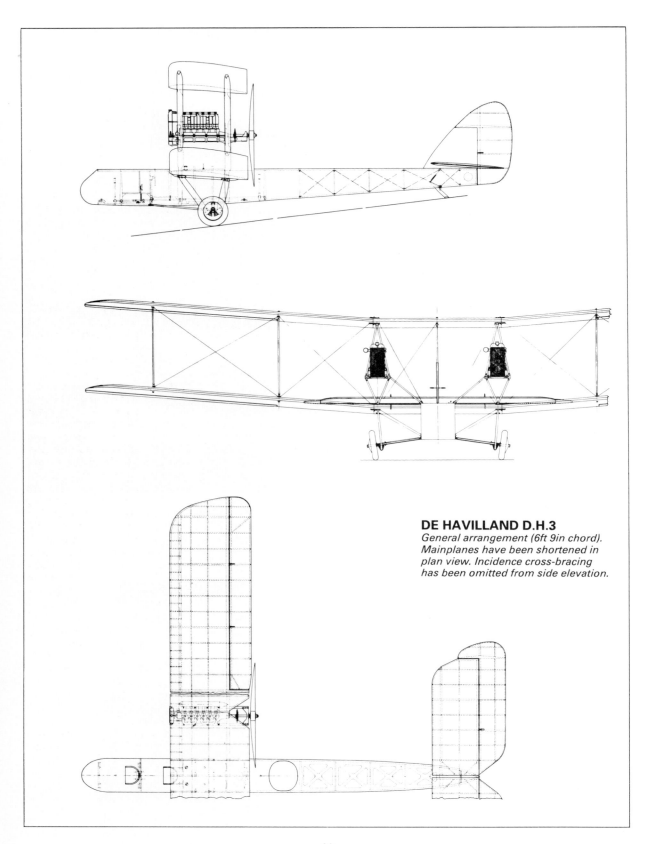

DE HAVILLAND D.H.3
General arrangement (6ft 9in chord).
Mainplanes have been shortened in
plan view. Incidence cross-bracing
has been omitted from side elevation.

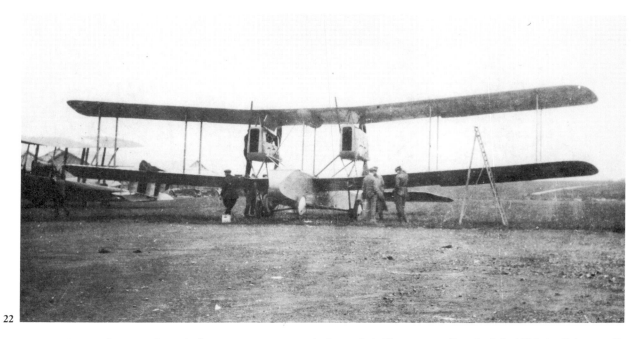

22

more engine can be seen: these shafts were fitted to enable the propellers to clear the trailing edges of the wings.

By May 1916, when the D.H.3 went to Central Flying School to undergo official tests, it had acquired tall exhaust stacks and its engines were more extensively cowled. Photograph 22, taken at the CFS, includes (at left) the first F.E.4, which, although somewhat similar to the D.H.3, had a greatly inferior performance. Damage sustained by the D.H.3 apparently delayed its testing until early July 1916; its flying qualities were favourably reported on.

Although the D.H.3 was pleasant to fly, it was underpowered. It was therefore re-engined with two 160hp Beardmores, driving four-blade propellers. The extension shafts were abandoned, and consequently cutouts had to be made in the trailing edges of the mainplanes. Aerodynamic interference between the rotating propellers caused blade-tip flutter, to obviate which a surface (reported to be a sheet of plywood) was fitted to the rear central interplane strut. As photograph 23 shows, the balance area of the rudder was enlarged. In this form the aircraft was designated D.H.3A.

In photograph 24, the interpropeller surface of the D.H.3A appears to have been modified to an elliptical shape. Presumably it was this form of the design that was the subject of Contract No. 87/A/744 for fifty aircraft (A5088–A5137). This was given in September 1916, some ten weeks after the initial contract for the single-engine D.H.4 was signed. No production D.H.3 was ever completed, apparently owing to a change in official policy that preferred single-engine bombers to twin-engine types. The prototype was sent to the Southern Aircraft Repair Depot at Farnborough, where it was dismantled.

23

24

DE HAVILLAND D.H.4

Role: Two-seat fighter-reconnaissance and bomber aircraft.

Powerplant: 1 × 200hp BHP, 230hp Galloway Adriatic, 230hp Siddeley Puma, 200hp RAF 3a, 260hp Fiat A-12, 250hp Rolls-Royce Marks I–IV (Eagles I–IV), 275hp Rolls-Royce Marks I–III (Eagles V–VII) or 375hp Rolls-Royce Eagle VIII; (experimental) 1 × 200hp RAF 4d (A7864), 190hp Renault (A7726, A7751, B9488, B9494), 300hp Renault 12Fe (A2142), 353hp Rolls-Royce G (A7819), 260hp Sunbeam (Maori presumed), 400hp Sunbeam Matabele (A8083).

Armament: One fixed 0.303in Vickers machine gun (twin Vickers guns fitted on early Westland-built D.H.4s for RNAS), synchronized by Constantinesco CC gear (some aircraft had twin fixed overwing Lewis guns on the centre-section); one 0.303in Lewis gun, or a double-yoked pair, on Scarff ring mounting on rear cockpit; two 230lb or four 112lb bombs or equivalent. Experimental installations of Coventry Ordnance Works quick-firing gun were made on at least three aircraft (A2168, A7879 and A7894).

First flight: Mid-August 1916.

Contractors	Contract nos.	Serial nos.	Qty. ordered	Qty. delivered	Remarks
	C.P.151348/16	3696–3697	2	2	3697 briefly renumbered B394, March 1917.
	87/A/496	A2125–A2174	50	50	
Aircraft Mfg. Co.	87/A/496	A7401–A8090	690	683	A7559 became D.H.9 prototype under Contract A.S.17569. A8059, A8063, A8065, A8066, A8067 and A8069 transferred to Contract A.S.41996.
	87/A/496	B1482	1	1	Additional aircraft under 87/A/496. Had RAF 3a engine.
F.W. Berwick	87/A/1185	B2051–B2150	100	100	
Westland	A.S.29679 [C.P.101977/17]	B3955–B3968 (see under N5960–N6009)	–	13	Transferred from RNAS. B3968 cancelled.
	A.S.29679 [C.P.103711/17]	B3987 (see under N6380–N6429)	–	1	Replaced B3968.
Vulcan	87/A/1413	B5451–B5550	100	100	
Westland	A.S.29679 [C.P.103711/17]	B9434–B9439, B9456, B9458, B9460, B9461, B9470 (see under N6380–N6429)	–	11	
	A.S.29679	B9476–B9500	25	25	
Vulcan	A.S.17570/17	C1051–C1150	100	–	Cancelled. Numbers re-allocated for S.E.5as.
Aircraft Mfg. Co.	A.S.24960	C4501–C4540	40	40	Originally ordered (50) by Russia with Fiat engines. Ten converted to spares.
Westland	A.S.29679	D1751–D1775	25	25	
	A.S.37726	D8351–D8430	80	79	D8408 transferred to Ctt.35a/680/C.553.
	A.S.41996	D9231–D9280	50	49	See note against A7401–A8090. D9231 transferred to Ctt.35a/680/C.553.
Aircraft Mfg. Co.	35a/216/C.127	E4624–E4628	5	5	
	A.S.37726	F1551	1	1	To replace D8408 (see above).
	87/A/496	F1552	1	1	To replace D9231 (see above).
Glendower	35a/660/C.540	F2633–F2732	100	100	Without mainplanes and ailerons.
Palladium	35a/669/C.544	F5699–F5798	100	100	
Aircraft Mfg. Co.	35a/1692/C.1795	F7597, F7598	2	2	
Glendower	35a/2121/C.2511	H5290	1	1	
Palladium	35a/2556/C.2849	H5894–H5939	46	46	
	35a/2149/C.2512	H8263	1	1	Built as sample airframe but converted for service. Serial no. allotted 26 September 1918.
Westland	C.P.101977/17	N5960–N6009	50	50	N5970, '80, '86, '87, '90, '91, '94, '95, '98, '99, N6002, '03, '06 to RFC as B3955–B3967 (N6007 should have become B3968 but was destroyed by fire 1 Oct. 1917).
Westland	C.P.103711/17	N6380–N6429	50	50	N6380, N6382–N6387, N6393, N6397, N6401, '05, '09 to RFC, as B3987, B9434–B9439, B9456, B9458, B9460, B9461, B9470.

Geoffrey de Havilland's first truly great design was the D.H.4. Initially intended to have the 160hp Beardmore engine, it was modified to take advantage of the new 200hp BHP. A handsome two-bay biplane, it made its first flight in mid-August 1916 and in the following month went to the Central Flying School, where photograph **25** was taken. Testing of the D.H.4 was conducted between 21 September and 12 October 1916 and the aircraft was given an excellent assessment. From Upavon it flew direct to France on 15 October.

On 17 October 1916 Geoffrey de Havilland wrote to Major-General Trenchard, telling him that a second

25

prototype, powered by a 250hp Rolls-Royce engine, was expected to be ready for flight by the following weekend (21/22 October) and that several modifications would be incorporated in later D.H.4s. The second prototype, seen in photograph **26** at Hendon, had a revised engine installation that lowered the power

unit to improve the pilot's forward view; the wings were positioned further forward and the disposition of the centre-section struts was altered accordingly; and redesigned undercarriage V-struts were employed.

The rear cockpit opening on the second prototype differed visibly from that of the first and was ob-

viously intended to permit the installation of a rotating mounting for the observer's Lewis gun. The D.H.4 was so much faster than any contemporary two-seater that it was thought doubtful whether an observer could effectively use such a weapon installation at combat speeds. In November 1916 the second prototype had the top

26

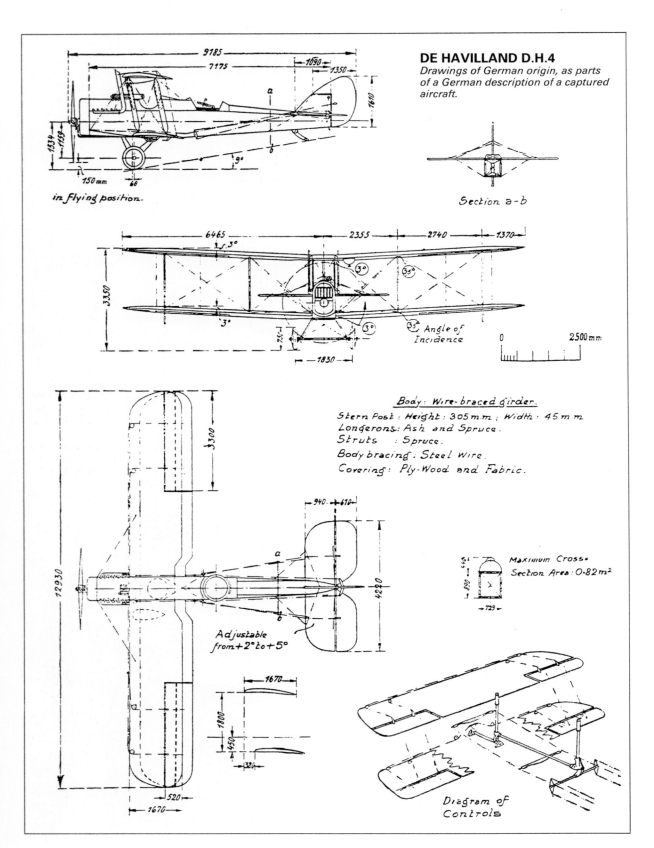

DE HAVILLAND D.H.4

Drawings of German origin, as parts of a German description of a captured aircraft.

9785

7175

1090

1350

1670

1534
1459

a

b

150 mm

9°

6°

in flying position.

Section a-b

6465

2355

2740

1370

5°3°

3°

3°

3°

3°

5°

5°

3°

7·5°

3350

1830

5° Angle of Incidence

0   2500 mm

Body: Wire-braced girder.
Stern Post: Height: 305 m.m.; Width: 45 m.m.
Longerons: Ash and Spruce.
Struts   : Spruce.
Body bracing: Steel wire.
Covering: Ply-Wood and Fabric.

3300

940   670

a

b

4220

12930

Adjustable
from +2° to +5°

Maximum Cross-
Section Area: 0·82 m²

729

1670

1800

450

1336

520

1670

Diagram of
Controls

24

27

28

production D.H.4s had the Scarff No. 2 ring mounting as standard.

Typifying the earliest production form of the D.H.4, A2129 was sent to Orfordness, the locale for photograph **28**. It had a 250hp Rolls-Royce engine, probably a Mark III (Eagle III), and is seen fully armed, with the pilot's Vickers gun on the forward decking immediately ahead of the cockpit, offset to port; the Type A trigger motor of its Constantinesco CC gear is just visible. The observer's Scarff ring mounting is placed directly on the upper longerons. This D.H.4 made two defensive sorties on 13 June 1917 against the Gotha formation that attacked London that day but evidently did not succeed in joining combat with the enemy bombers.

The first batches of D.H.4s to be delivered to the RNAS were built by F. W. Petter's Westland Aircraft Works at Yeovil. These aircraft had twin Vickers guns for the pilot, and the observer's use of his Scarff-mounted Lewis gun was made more effective by raising the ring mounting to the level of the top of the upper decking. The rounded top decking was retained at this time, and the space under the ring mounting was neatly faired over with plywood. The subject of photograph **29** is N5972, which was in 'A' Flight of No. 2 (Naval) Squadron early in February 1918. At that time it had a 275hp

decking about the rear cockpit modified to the shape seen in photograph **27**; it was designed to act as a wind deflector for the observer. Two separate gun mountings were installed. The forward one was simply a fixed pillar; the rear resembled the Anderson mounting employed on the F.E.2b and its gun was to have a compensating sight of unspecified type. This arrangement was tested at Orfordness, where photograph 27 was taken (at the time the aircraft had the enigmatic marking 'GX D4' on its rudder), but fortunately this primitive installation was not adopted and

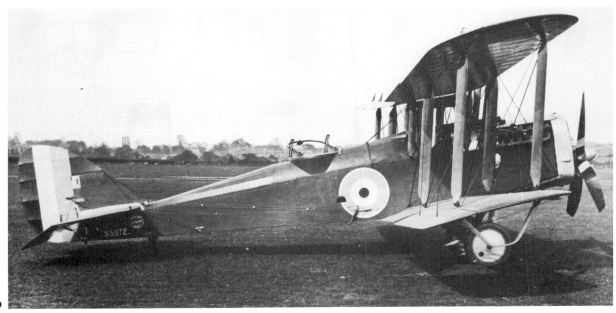

29

Rolls-Royce Mark I, or Eagle V, No.5/Eagle/116, but by 30 March that had been replaced by an Eagle VI. Photograph **30** depicts a busy scene at Petite-Synthe as bombed-up D.H.4s of No. 5 (Naval) Squadron are made ready for take-off. The nearest aircraft is Westland-built and has the elevated Scarff ring with fairings on the observer's cockpit. It also has narrow stripes on the radiator cowling, presumably a Flight marking.

Early in June 1917 it was arranged that the RNAS would transfer D.H.4s to the RFC at the rate of two per week, on the understanding that they would be replaced at a later date. It was reported that two were ready for transfer on 6 June 1917 and that the first, B3955, was to be flown to RFC Headquarters in France at once. The aircraft concerned were all Westland-built, and a total of 25 were transferred in the process: they were renumbered in the process, B3955 having originally been N5970. It was delayed by minor damage but, repaired, it was reallocated on 28 June, and went to No. 55 Squadron. On 7 July 1917 it was sent to No. 1 Aircraft Depot, St-Omer, but returned to No. 55 to give months

30

31

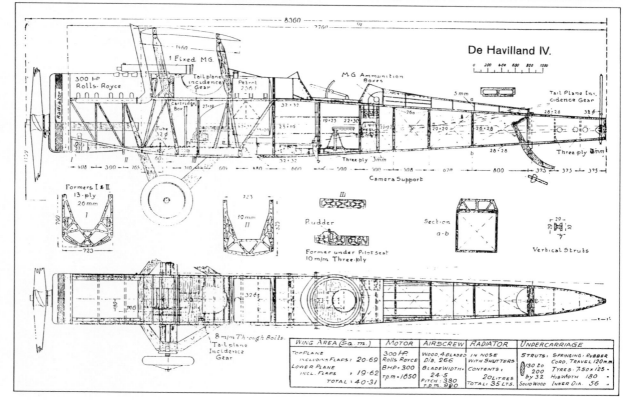

De Havilland IV.

WING AREA (Sq. m.)		MOTOR	AIRSCREW	RADIATOR	UNDERCARRIAGE	
TOP PLANE INCLUDING FLAPS:	20·69	300 H.P. Rolls Royce	WOOD, 4-BLADED DIA. 266	IN NOSE WITH SHUTTERS	STRUTS: SPRINGING: RUBBER	CORD. TRAVEL 120 m.m.
LOWER PLANE INCL. FLAPS	19·62	BHP: 300	BLADE WIDTH: 24·5	CONTENTS:	30 to 200 by 32	TYRES: 750 x 125 · HUB WIDTH 180 ·
TOTAL:	40·31	r.p.m. 1650	PITCH: 330 r.p.m. 990	20 LITRES TOTAL: 35 LTS.	SOLID WOOD	INNER DIA. 56 "

of operational service before being struck off charge on 17 May 1918. It was the official intention that these transferred ex-RNAS D.H.4s should be issued to Training Brigade in preference to the standard RFC form of D.H.4, and most did go to training units. B3960 (ex-N5991) was photographed at Scampton (**31**), possibly as a visiting aircraft. In November 1917 it was with No. 44 Training Squadron, Waddington. When photographed it had a distinctive unit marking on the fuselage.

N6000, a Westland-built D.H.4 of No. 5 (Naval) Squadron is seen at Petite-Synthe in photographs **32** and **33**. It had retained its twin-Vickers armament but had the revised, square-section top decking on the rear fuselage. When photographed it had a single 112lb bomb under the fuselage and eight 25lb Cooper bombs, four under each lower wing. The tricolour stripes on the elevators were unusual for a D.H.4. N6000 was with No. 5 (Naval) Squadron by mid-September 1917 and was frequently flown by Flight Lieutenant C. P. O. Bartlett on many of the squadron's bombing missions. By 3 January 1918 it had an Eagle VI engine, No.2/275/236, and

was still on the strength of the BEF on 30 June 1918.

The remarkable variety of engines that were fitted to the D.H.4 led to daunting problems and many delays in the production shop of the Aircraft Manufacturing Co. while the batch A7401–A8090 was going through. Engines apparently were fitted as they became available, more or less regardless of type, and airframes had to be adapted to accept them. Even different marks of Rolls-Royce engine called for different design details in the fuselage. By June 1917 the firm had succeeded in modifying the fuse-

SQN. LDR. C. P. O. BARTLETT DSC

32

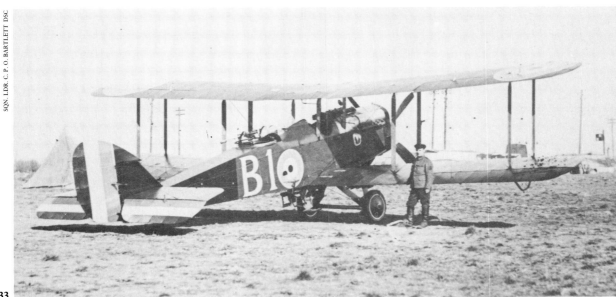

SQN. LDR. C. P. O. BARTLETT DSC

33

lage to be capable of accepting any mark of Rolls-Royce Eagle, and the first D.H.4 of this type was A7446 (photograph **34**), which arrived at Martlesham Heath on 9 August 1917, fitted with an early 375hp Eagle VIII that itself was considered to be experimental and apparently had no number. After exhaustive testing A7446 returned to the manufacturer on 17 September and on 19 October it was officially allocated to the Expeditionary Force. On the previous day, 18 October, the RNAS had requested twenty D.H.4s fitted with Eagle VIII engines and with large cameras 'for special work'. Perhaps coincidentally, the RFC lent A7446 to

the RNAS and the aircraft was with No. 2 (Naval) Squadron by 5 January 1918. It was formally allocated to RNAS Dunkerque on 15 March 1918 and remained in No. 202 Squadron RAF. It was last reported at No. 4 Aeroplane Supply Depot, Guines, on 25 October 1918.

In No. 202 Squadron RAF the Eagle-powered D.H.4 saw regular use as a fighter-reconnaissance aircraft. The D.H.4s of 'A' Flight constituted the squadron's photographic element and some of them had cameras of such length that a ventral fairing had to be fitted round the protruding end of the camera body. This is clearly visible in the fine study of A7845 (photograph

35), which had first gone to No. 2 (Naval) Squadron from Dover on 2 January 1918. On 30 March 1918 its engine was a Rolls-Royce Eagle VIII, No.8/Eagle/136. The aircraft had to go to No. 4 ASD at a later date and was re-issued to No. 202 Squadron on 28 June 1918. As a later-production D.H.4 it had the taller Mark II undercarriage. A8025, also of No. 202 Squadron and similarly fitted with an Eagle VIII engine (No.8/Eagle/134), had no camera fairing but had supplementary armament consisting of two fixed Lewis guns on the centre-section (photograph **36**). It may have been in 'C' Flight, known in No. 202 Squadron as the Escort Flight. Unfortu-

T. J. HEFFERNAN

34

35

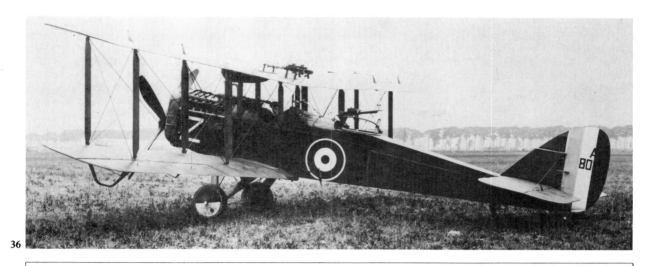

36

D.H.4 UNITS, BASES AND MARKINGS (BRITISH)

OPERATIONAL UNITS (RFC/RAF)

Squadron	Bases	Sqn. markings
18	Baizieux, La Belle Vue, Auchel, Treizennes, Serny, Maisoncelle	White square on fuselage side abaft roundel
25	Lozinghem, Boisdinghem, Serny, Villers-Bretonneux, Beauvois, Ruisseauville, La Brayelle	White crescent, in supine attitude, on fuselage side abaft roundel
27	Clairmarais, Serny, Villers-Bretonneux, Beauvois, Ruisseauville, Fourneuil, Ruisseauville, Chailly, Beauvois	White vertical bar on fuselage side abaft roundel
30	Baquba, Qubba, Baquba, Kifri, Baquba	None known
49	La Belle Vue, Les Eauvis, Boisdinghem, Petite-Synthe	White dumb-bell on fuselage side midway between roundel and l/e of tailplane
55	Fienvillers, Boisdinghem, Ochey, Tantonville, Azelot, Le Planty, St-André-aux-Bois	White equilateral triangle immediately behind roundel on fuselage side
57	Fienvillers, Droglandt, Boisdinghem, Ste-Marie-Cappel, Le Quesnoy-en-Artois, Vert Galant, Spa, Spy	White disc on fuselage side immediately abaft roundel
63	Basra	None known
72	Samarra	None known

OPERATIONAL UNITS (RNAS)

No. 2 Sqn. (later 202 RAF), Bergues; No. 5 Sqn. (later 205 RAF), Petite-Synthe, Villers-Bretonneux, Mons-en-Chaussée, Champien, Bertangles, Bois de Roche, Bovelles, Proyart East, Moislains, Maubeuge, La Louveterie; No. 6 Sqn. (later 206 RAF), Dover, Petite-Synthe; No. 11 Sqn. (later 211 RAF), Petite-Synthe; No. 12 Sqn. (later 212 RAF), Coudekerque; No. 17 Sqn. (later 217 RAF), St-Pol; 'A' Sqn. (later 222 RAF), Thasos; 'C' Sqn. (later 220 RAF), Imbros (Gliki); 'D' Sqn. (later 221 RAF), Stavros; No. 2 Wing, Mudros; No. 6 Wing, Otranto.

RAF SQUADRONS

Nos. 220–222 (See RNAS Sqns. 'A', 'C' and 'D'); No. 223, Mudros; No. 224 (Flts. Nos. 496, 497 and 498), Otranto; No. 226, Pizzone; No. 227, Pizzone; No. 233, Dover; No. 273, Yarmouth, Burgh Castle, Covehithe; No. 6 Group, Taranto; No. 15 Group, Mudros; RAF Contingent, Archangel.

SQUADRONS MOBILIZING

No. 49, Dover; No. 83, Spittlegate; No. 121, Narborough.

TRAINING UNITS (RFC/RAF)

No. 9 TS, Norwich, Sedgeford; No. 18 TS, Montrose; No. 19 TS, Hounslow, The Curragh; No. 31 TS, Wyton; No. 44 TS, Harlaxton, Waddington; No. 46 TS, Catterick; No. 51 TS, Waddington; No. 52 TS, Catterick; No. 61 TS, South Carlton; No. 69 TS, Bramham Moor; No. 75 TS, Cramlington.

TRAINING DEPOT STATIONS

No. 2, Stonehenge; No. 6, Boscombe Down; No. 7, Feltwell; No. 9, Shawbury; No. 10, Harling Road; No. 11, Old Sarum; No. 14, Lake Down, Boscombe Down; No. 15, Hucknall; No. 31, Fowlmere; No. 35, Duxford; No. 49, Catterick; No. 52, Cramlington; No. 57, Cranwell; No. 58, Cranwell.

OTHER TRAINING UNITS

Schools of Navigation & Bomb Dropping: No. 1, Stonehenge; No. 2, Andover; No. 4, Thetford.
Schools of Aerial Fighting and Gunnery: No. 2, Marske; No. 3, Bircham Newton; No. 4 (Auxiliary), Marske.
No. 1 (Observers') School of Aerial Gunnery, New Romney.
Artillery and Infantry Co-operation School, Worthy Down.
School for Anti-Submarine Inshore Patrol Observers, Aldeburgh.
Day & Night Bombing and Observation School, Lympne.
Fleet School of Aerial Fighting and Gunnery, East Fortune.
Marine Observers' School, Leysdown.
Observers' Schools, No. 1 at Eastchurch, No. 2 at Manstone.
School of Photography, Farnborough.

RNAS TRAINING STATIONS

Cranwell: Manstone D.H.4 School; Eastchurch; Turnhouse Fleet Base.

37

38

39

40

nately, this D.H.4 was lost on 28 September 1918 when it ran out of fuel and came down in enemy territory. Captain A. V. Bowater and Lieutenant Malvin became prisoners of war.

Six Eagle-Fours of No. 217 Squadron RAF are shown lined up on their aerodrome in photograph **37**. All have distinctive markings on their radiator cowlings and wheel covers, while the nearest aircraft, F5721, and its neighbour have a 230lb bomb under the fuselage. As one of the units of the 61st Wing RAF, No. 217's work was with naval forces and was primarily anti-submarine. On 12 August 1918 four of its D.H.4s, led by Captain K. G. Boyd, dropped eight 230lb bombs on a U-boat and sank it off Ostend. F5721 remained in service after the Armistice; on 26 April 1919 it went to No. 2 Communications Squadron at Buc for what was described as 'special duty with HM The King of the Belgians'.

As if in some atavistic reflection of the experimental rear armament tried out on the second prototype D.H.4 (see photograph 26), A7848 at Great Yarmouth had two Lewis guns on separate pillar mountings on the rear cockpit, as shown in photograph **38**. Several other D.H.4s at Yarmouth

were similarly armed, including A8032, on which Major E. Cadbury and Captain R. Leckie shot down the Zeppelin L.70 on 5 August 1918. A7848 itself had made a defensive sortie in the early hours of 13 April 1918 against the L.62; it was flown by Squadron Commander Vincent Nicholl but made no contact. Its fuselage marking more probably represented the number 11 than any unit insignia: two other contemporary D.H.4s at Yarmouth bore the numerals '1' and '3' without additional markings.

At the time when the Royal Air Force was formed by amalgamating the RFC and the RNAS there were at Great Yarmouth two Eagle-powered D.H.4s that in contemporary records were annotated as 'Special Service'. One was A7848, the other A7830; both had as rear armament two pillar-mounted Lewis guns. A7830 was transferred to the Controller of the Technical Department on 16 July 1918, and it was probably after that date that it was given the dazzle-painting scheme seen in photograph **39**, which was taken at the Isle of Grain. Later, the undersides of the mainplanes were painted with multiple sinuously curving patterns in a dark colour.

In the light of the D.H.4's operational history, it now seems odd that early official thinking did not at first regard the Rolls-Royce-powered version as suitable for bombing duties: indeed, it had been decided that it would be used as a fighter-reconnaissance aircraft and that those D.H.4s destined for bombing duties would be powered by the RAF 3a and BHP (Adriatic/Puma) engines. The first Eagle-Fours supplied to No. 55 Squadron (paradoxically, it would seem: No. 55 was intended to be a bomber unit) were delivered without bomb racks in accordance with that philosophy, which apparently had not been confided to RFC Headquarters. A7624, the subject of photograph **40**, had, at least initially, a 275hp Rolls-Royce Mark I (Eagle V) engine. It was first allocated to the RFC in France on 3 September 1917, when it was still at Hendon Aircraft Acceptance Park. It was allocated to No. 55 Squadron RFC and is here seen as aircraft 'M' of that well-known unit, displaying the squadron's marking of a white equilateral triangle. This D.H.4 was later used by No. 99 Squadron as one of its mail-carrying aircraft in the post-Armistice period.

Little is known about the experimental floatplane version of an Eagle-powered D.H.4 depicted in photograph **41**, but it is believed that it was flown at Felixstowe. Its twin floats, long enough to render a tail float unnecessary, may have been inspired by those of the formidable German Brandenburg seaplane fighters with which Felixstowe's flying-boat pilots were more familiar than they would have wished.

Although the order for 690 D.H.4s placed with the Aircraft Manufacturing Co. was one of the largest of its time, it led to serious problems of engine supply. Despite utilizing every available Rolls-Royce engine, including modified pusher engines from F.E.2ds, supply fell short of demand. BHP engines encountered problems in production and were slow to come forward in worthwhile numbers, and consequently the RAF 3a was adopted as an alternative powerplant for the D.H.4. The first installation of an RAF 3a was made in A2168, which had been allocated to the Controller of the Technical Department for testing on 6 April 1917. Later that month it was tested at Martlesham Heath, the locale for photograph **42**. By 12 August it was at the Armament Experimental Station, Orfordness; although the aircraft was allocated to the RFC with the Expeditionary Force on 17 September 1917 its transfer was cancelled the next day. A2168 was subsequently used in tests of the Coventry Ordnance Works gun (see photograph **48**).

41

E. F. CHEESMAN

42

32

Redesign and the making of essential fittings delayed the delivery of production D.H.4s with the RAF 3a engine. Although the 3a was still an unknown quantity – the discovery of its weaknesses still lay in the future – the RNAS specifically asked for two RAF-powered D.H.4s on 5 June 1917, offering in exchange two Westland-built aircraft with Rolls-Royce engines. This was immediately agreed, despite the RFC's anxiety to get its hands on as many D.H.4s as

it could: perhaps the prospect of two Rolls-Royce engines expedited the Corps' acceptance. The RNAS wanted the RAF-powered aircraft for a projected photographic reconnaissance of the Kiel Canal that summer. To meet this need, A7457 and A7459 were selected and were recorded at RNAS Hendon 'for Special Service' on 12 June 1917: they were virtually the first production RAF 3a D.H.4s. For their projected flight they were specially camouflaged in matt-finish

sky blue and buff. The two views of A7459 (photographs **43** and **44**) illustrate this unusual finish, and also provide a clear image of the RAF 3a engine installation, characterized by a single central exhaust stack. The Kiel project was abandoned in mid-August 1917 and the two special D.H.4s were reallocated. A7459 was sent to Great Yarmouth for anti-airship operations in co-operation with flying boats. For this task the pilot's armament was increased by the addition of two fixed

43

44

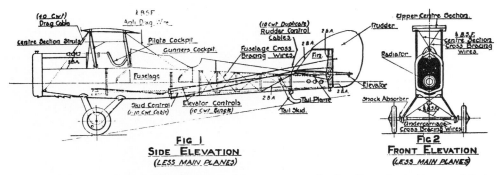

FIG 1
SIDE ELEVATION
(LESS MAIN PLANES)

FIG 2
FRONT ELEVATION
(LESS MAIN PLANES)

Flying Position. The Machine is in Flying Position when the Top Longerons directly in rear of the Engine are level longitudinally and transversely.

Truing up the Fuselage. Tension all Internal Cross Bracing Wires making corresponding diagonals equal & check by trammel. By means of Top Cross Bracing Wires true up until mid points of all Top Cross Struts are in line. Check by stretching a-line from the vertical centre line of front of Fuselage to axis of Rudderpost. Mark points on Front Vertical Side Struts 16⅝" vertically below the Top face of the Top Longerons (in the case of the R.A.F. 3a & 200 B.H.P. the measurement should be 15⅜"). Tension the Side Bracing Wires on one side until all the mid points of Side Struts of the Rear Portion and the marked point on the Front Side Strut, on that side, are in line & proceed similarly for the other side. Check by stretching two lines one each side, from front marked points to rear marked points. Make Bottom Cross Bracing Wires equal in each Bay. Place a Straightledge transversely across the Top Longerons immediately in

rear of Front Portion. Place another straightledge across the Top Longerons at any other point. The upper edge of the second straightledge should be in line with the Upper edge of the first straightledge. Check by sighting & repeat for other points.

Truing up the Undercarriage. Adjust the Front Cross Bracing Wires making corresponding diagonals equal & check by trammel.

Truing up Centre Section. The Centre Section must be symmetrical about the vertical centre line of Machine. Adjust Front Cross Bracing Wires making corresponding diagonals equal. Check for symmetry by dropping two plumb lines, one each side, from forward ends of extreme bolt Holes on Fish Plates. These plumb lines should be the same distance off their respective sides of the Fuselage. Adjust the Front Drag & Rear Anti Drag Cables until the stagger of the Centre Section is 12". Check by measuring the horizontal fore & aft distance between above mentioned plumb lines & the forward edges of bolts in Outer Holes on Attachments for Front Spars of Lower Main Planes.

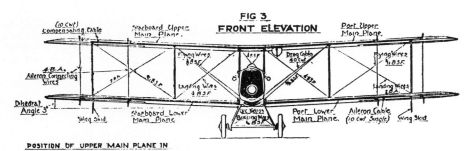

FIG 3
FRONT ELEVATION

POSITION OF UPPER MAIN PLANE IN RELATION TO LOWER MAIN PLANE.

FIG 4

DE HAVILLAND D.H.4 (275hp Rolls-Royce)

Official rigging diagrams (continued opposite). These should not be assumed to be dimensionally precise, but they are of interest for what they are and for their textual content.

TRUING UP MAIN PLANES

Dihedral. The Dihedral angle is 3° for both Upper and Lower Main Planes. Check by Abney level and straightledge along the Spars.

Incidence. The Incidence of the Main Planes is 3° throughout. Check by Abney level and straightledge, placing latter from Leading Edge to Trailing Edge at Rib.

Stagger. The Stagger of the Main Planes is 12" throughout. Check by measuring the horizontal fore and aft distances between Leading Edge of Lower Main Planes and plumb lines dropped from Leading Edge of Upper Main Planes. This measurement should be 12".

Ailerons. With Pilots Control Stick central the Droop of the Ailerons is 1". Check, for Main Planes being square with Machine, by taking measurements from the Bottom Sockets of Front Outer Struts to the Rudderpost, and corresponding points on the Front Drag Cable Wiring Plates. Corresponding measurements should be the same on both sides.

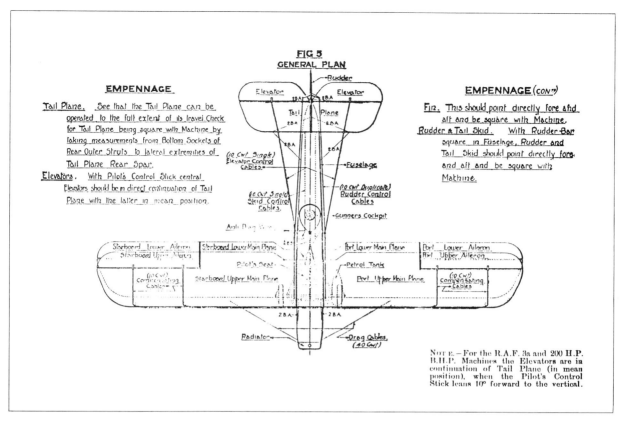

FIG 5
GENERAL PLAN

EMPENNAGE.

Tail Plane. See that the Tail Plane can be operated to the full extent of its travel. Check for Tail Plane being square with Machine by taking measurements from Bottom Sockets of Rear Outer Struts to lateral extremities of Tail Plane Rear Spar.

Elevators. With Pilot's Control Stick central Elevators should be in direct continuation of Tail Plane with the latter in mean position.

EMPENNAGE (CONT?)

Fin. This should point directly fore and aft and be square with Machine.

Rudder & Tail Skid. With Rudder-Bar square in Fuselage, Rudder and Tail Skid should point directly fore and aft and be square with Machine.

Rudder
Elevator
Elevator
Tail Plane
(10 Cwt Single) Elevator Control Cables
Fuselage
(10 cwt Duplicate) Rudder Control Cables
(10 Cwt Single) Skid Control Cables
Gunners Cockpit
Anti Drag Wires
Starboard Lower Aileron
Starboard Upper Aileron
Starboard Lower Main Plane
Port Lower Main Plane
Port Lower Aileron
Port Upper Aileron
(10 Cwt) Compensating Cables
Pilot's Seat
Petrol Tank
Starboard Upper Main Plane
Port Upper Main Plane
(10 Cwt) Compensating Cables
2 B A
2 B A
Radiator
Drag Cables (40 Cwt)

NOTE.— For the R.A.F. 3a and 200 H.P. B.H.P. Machines the Elevators are in continuation of Tail Plane (in mean position), when the Pilot's Control Stick leans 10° forward to the vertical.

Lewis guns above the centre-section; these were relatively widely spaced, being mounted directly above the centre-section struts. On 5 September 1917, after attacking the Zeppelin L.44, A7459 suffered engine failure and Flight Lieutenant A. H. H. Gilligan and Lieutenant G. S. Trewin had to ditch. They were rescued by the accompanying Curtiss H-12 No. 8666 but the flying boat was then unable to take off and drifted for three days before being found and retrieved. The D.H.4 sank and was lost.

A7457 was allocated to RNAS Grain on 24 September 1917 and arrived there six days later. Dated 28 January 1918, photograph **45** records the aircraft's installation of inflatable air bags, with a biplane hydrovane fitted in front of the wheels (which were jettisonable) and wing-tip floats under the lower wings. A successful

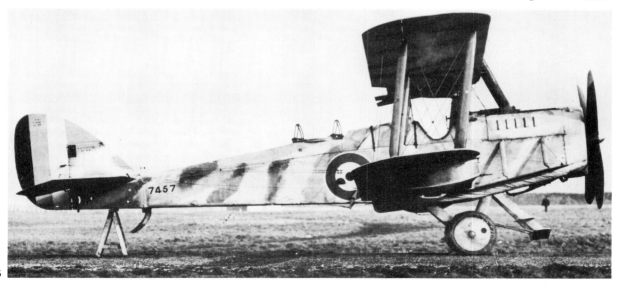

45

35

46

47

ditching with this emergency flotation gear was photographed on 29 March 1918, though the event had probably been preceded by trials. By 5 January 1918 A7457 had the RAF 3a engine No. 6605, and by 30 March the aircraft was officially recorded on the strength of Grain's Type Test Flight.

Despite the quite serious shortcomings of the RAF 3a engine, D.H.4s to which it was fitted were sent to unlikely places. The RAF-powered D.H.4 seen in photograph

46 (taken in the Middle East) is believed to be one of the few that were used by No. 63 Squadron. Of these, A8005 is known to have been with the squadron in November 1918. The aircraft that went to North Russia with the RAF Contingent in the late summer of 1918 included eight D.H.4s with RAF 3a engines. In photograph 47, A7919 is seen bombed-up in preparation for a mission.

A2168 (see also photograph 42) was

used, later in its career, in experiments with the Coventry Ordnance Works 37mm automatic gun that fired 1½lb shells; it is depicted in this configuration in photograph 48. The aircraft retained its RAF 3a engine, the central exhaust stack of which was replaced by a long pipe that was led along the starboard side of the aircraft to a point abaft the rear cockpit. The fuselage structure must have been greatly strengthened to withstand the heavy recoil of the gun, and the

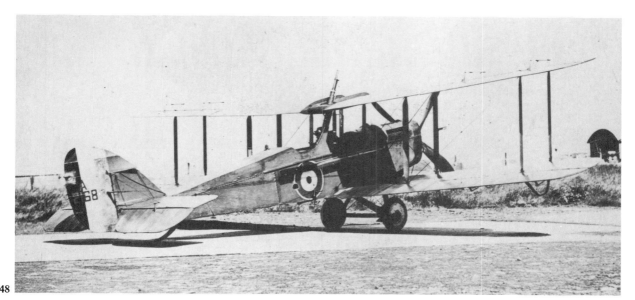

centre-section was cut away to let the long barrel pass through. The high elevation of the gun suggests that it was intended to be used as an anti-airship weapon, or perhaps to attack formations of enemy bombers from below. Two other D.H.4s, A7879 and A7894, were fitted with COW guns. The precise form of their installations is not known, but both aircraft had Rolls-Royce Eagle III engines; they may have been the two COW-gun-armed D.H.4s reported to have gone

to France in November 1918. On 2 December both were allocated to the South-Eastern Area for the Controller of the Technical Department.

The standard installation of the Siddeley Puma in the D.H.4 is seen in photograph **49** on the Westland-built D1769, which had been the first of its batch to be fitted with the Mark II undercarriage. It was allocated to RNAS Grain on 22 January 1918 for experimental purposes and arrived there four days later. By 3 May 1918

it had been fitted with Grain flotation gear, a biplane hydrovane on the undercarriage and wing-tip floats; by mid-August a simplified, monoplane hydrovane had replaced its complex biplane predecessor. Later, D1769 reverted to a standard wheel under-carriage and participated in Major Orde Lees's experiments with para-chutes. Two Calthrop Guardian Angel static-line parachutes were stowed into special cavities formed in the underside of the fuselage between the cockpits. The D.H.4 made dummy drops, using a deactivated bomb as a sinker weight, and Major Orde Lees made at least one live drop from the aircraft. For trials with and without the parachutes D1769 went to Martlesham Heath late in October 1918 and left that station on 2 November. Also Westland-built, N6416 (photograph 50) was another Puma-powered D.H.4. Late in October 1917 it was at Manstone (today's Manston), but by 1 February 1918 it was with No. 2 Wing RNAS, Mudros, as one of sixteen Puma-Fours that were then on strength (together with three Rolls-Royce engines and three engineless airframes; all but four were being assembled at that time). N6416 was still at Imbros in July 1918 and acquired the striking 'sun-burst' paint scheme seen in the photograph.

On some Puma-powered D.H.4s the exhaust pipe had a downward-angled outlet, as seen in photograph 51, but the aircraft depicted also has the four-blade propeller of type A.M.1329 that usually denoted a Galloway Adriatic engine rather than a Siddeley Puma. Although of the same basic design, these two engines were by no means identical and there was virtually no interchangeability

TIM MASON

50

between them. The unidentified D.H.4 shown has a distinctly used look and probably belonged to a training unit in Britain. It had been decided, earlier than 13 September 1917, that D.H.4s with the Galloway engine were not to be sent to France.

The installation of the 260hp Fiat A.12 engine in the D.H.4 was made for use in the batch of 50 aircraft that were ordered by the Russian government. The first such installation was made in A7532, which arrived at Martlesham Heath for performance trials on 30 June 1917. Its evaluation completed, it left Martlesham for

Hounslow on 9 August. No Fiat-powered D.H.4 was ready for dispatch to Russia before ice closed the sea lanes to Russian ports; and the revolution of that winter prevented subsequent deliveries. Forty of the aircraft were taken over by the RFC as C4501–C4540, the remaining ten being delivered as spares. The engine installations were made at the Southern Aircraft Repair Depot, Farnborough, but as late as 25 October 1917 it was reported that 200 necessary parts were still lacking. This D.H.4 variant was used operationally by No. 49 Squadron: despite the lack

RAF MUSEUM P10242

51

of the 200 parts, all forty aircraft had been officially allocated to the RFC in France on 19 October 1917, though it is unlikely that C4503, C4519 or C4539 ever went there. Known allocations to No. 49 Squadron were made in February and March 1918, and at least nine Fiat-Fours survived to be flown back to England between 1 April and 25 July 1918; C4521 was reported to be on charge of the Independent Force as late as 10 October 1918. Photograph 52, showing a Fiat-Four, was taken at a training unit in England, possibly at Wyton.

As early as 29 December 1916 **52** *Colonel* Régnier, *Directeur de l'Aéronautique Militaire*, wrote on behalf of the French Minister of War to Major-General Trenchard, requesting a specimen D.H.4. Trenchard replied on 3 January 1917 that he had asked the War Office to release one of the first ten D.H.4s to the French government. The selected aircraft was A2142, which on 30 January 1917 had been allocated to No. 55 Squadron RFC while still at Hendon. On 11 February it was struck off the strength of the RFC and was flown to Paris by Captain Dunn, who was to hand it over to a French officer. In photograph **53**, A2142 is seen at

Villacoublay, fitted with a Renault engine, possibly a 300hp 12Fe. Early in September 1917, at the request of the Military Aeronautics Directorate, another D.H.4, A7647, was flown to France by Captain B. C. Hucks, to be used in tests with what was reported as a 280hp Renault engine (possibly a 12Fby or 12Fcy). Curiously, these tests were to be conducted with, or by, the Farman company: perhaps the position of the Aircraft Manufacturing Company as the British licensee for the production of pre-war Farman types was relevant. Evidently

A7647 returned from its Renault experiments, for by 7 February 1918 it was with 'C' Flight of No.5 (Naval) Squadron at Dunkerque, fitted with a 275hp Rolls-Royce Mark III (Eagle VII) engine. Following a crash, the aircraft was deleted on 11 March 1918. Unconnected with these tests in France, the D.H.4s A7726, A7751, B9488 and B9494 were at RNAS Cranwell early in 1918, powered by 190hp Renault engines (presumably 8Gds or variants thereof). At that time Cranwell had five additional Renault engines of this type, all serviceable.

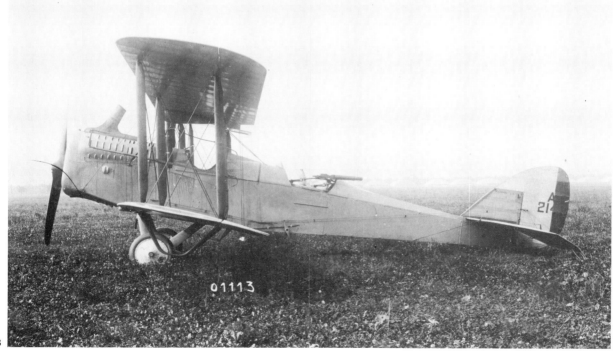

53

DE HAVILLAND D.H.4 (AMERICAN)

Role: Two-seat fighter-reconnaissance and bomber aircraft.
Powerplant: 1 × 400hp Liberty 12.
Armament: Two 0.3in Marlin machine guns synchronized by Nelson Gun Control; two 0.3in Lewis guns on Scarff ring mounting; bomb load.
First flight: February 1918.

Contractors*	Contract nos.*	Serial nos.	Qty. ordered	Qty. delivered	Remarks
Dayton-Wright	1816 (Order no. 20038-8)		4,000	3,098	
	(Order no. 20529-1)		2	2	One source quotes six delivered.
	(Order no. 20038-44)		1,000	–	
Fisher Body Corp.	218 (Order no. 20207-A)		4,000	1,600	
Standard Aircraft	2696–A (Order no. 20516-A)		500	140	

*Wartime contractors and contract numbers are shown. Figures of deliveries are unconfirmed; production periods have not been stated.

It might almost be said that the large-scale production of the D.H.4 in the USA occurred by default. On America's entry into the war in April 1917, an eleven-man commission headed by Major (later Colonel) Raynal Cawthorne Bolling was set up; its members sailed for Europe on 17 June 1917, intent on assessing European aircraft and engines with a view to their production in the USA. One of Bolling's earliest cables, dated 28 June 1917, advised the Chairman of the Aircraft Production Board (Howard E. Coffin) that a Camel, an S.E.5a and probably one D.H.4 would leave for the USA aboard the SS *Adriatic*. A specimen D.H.4 without an engine, probably A7531, arrived on 18 July 1917.

On 30 July General Pershing cabled the US Adjutant-General a list of French, British and Italian aircraft types recommended for American production. This included the D.H.4, subject to the opinion that some changes in design would be necessary to increase the bomb load. On 2 August Bolling cabled: 'British have already made changes suggested

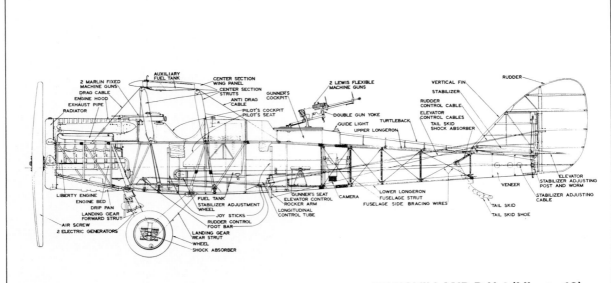

DE HAVILLAND D.H.4 (Liberty 12)
A fully detailed side elevation from the official Manual of Rigging Notes, Division of Military Aeronautics, USA.

D.H.4 and now call it D.H.9'. Evidently this news (and, doubtless, other relevant communications) sufficed to persuade the Aircraft Production Board to prefer the ostensibly improved design, for on 5 September 1917 the Board resolved to order, *inter alia*, '2,000 de Havilland 9s modified to receive U.S.12 [i.e. Liberty 12] aircraft engines': the *alia* did not include the D.H.4. Bolling was not impressed, and cabled the Chief Signal Officer on 26 September: 'We think number D.H.9 not sufficient suggest should be doubled'. The Board went even further: on 31 October 1917 it recommended that an existing contract on the Fisher Body Corporation be amended to call for 3,000 D.H.9s plus 1,000 D.H.9 fuselages and 1,500 sets of D.H.9 wings, and that the Dayton-Wright company should build 3,750 D.H.9s and 250 D.H.4s. These last two figures were further amended, on 6 November, to 3,000 and 1,000 respectively. On 15 January 1918 what appeared to be a contract for a further 1,000 D.H.9s from Fisher Body was recommended; and two days later 500 D.H.9s without engines were ordered from the Standard Aircraft Corporation.

It was originally intended to use the D.H.4s only as trainers, but by 25 January 1918 it was decided that, as the D.H.9 design was, in American

eyes, 'not yet sufficiently settled to permit production', 3,000 D.H.9s would be replaced by the same number of D.H.4s. This decision suggests that the Americans had no idea of the extensive commonality of components in the D.H.4 and D.H.9. On 12 February 1918 all American D.H.9 contracts were amended to call for D.H.4s; and under Production Program No. III of April 1918 the D.H.4 was 'transferred to combat classification for use in Europe'. It was intended to equip 24 observation squadrons and 44 day-bombing squadrons with the Liberty-powered D.H.4.

The first American-built D.H.4s were delivered in February 1918 by the Dayton-Wright Airplane Company, and production gathered momentum during 1918. Quoted figures of eventual output vary, probably because they related to differing periods of time, and there may have been confusion over contracts for spares or modifications. Totals of 3,151, 3,227 and 3,911 have been published. In 1940 a lecture entitled 'The Measure of America's World War Aeronautical Effort' was delivered at Norwich University under the James Jackson Cabot professorship by Colonel Edgar S. Gorrell. In this he presented a table of detailed statistics relating to American-built

D.H.4s, and these included the highest total of all:

Deliveries to US Government up to 31.12.18	4,587
Deliveries to US Government up to 11.11.18	3,431
Received overseas up to 11.11.18	1,213
D.H.4s with squadrons up to 11.11.18	499
D.H.4s actively used by squadrons up to 11.11.18	417

It is, of course, possible that Colonel Gorrell's total of 4,587 included spares-equivalents of airframes, which would be reasonable and, indeed, a truer reflection of the prodigious American production effort. Yet other figures suggest an improbable total of some 4,842. The precise total will perhaps never be known.

At least in the USAS bomber squadrons, the D.H.4 was not popular with its crews. Had the war lasted longer it would have been replaced by the USD-9A (see photographs 105–107), yet it was the D.H.4 that survived the Armistice to serve for some years in many varied forms and much-modified developments.

The American D.H.4 No. 32410 is seen in photograph **54**, probably taken at Villacoublay. It has bomb ribs under the lower wings and a wind-driven generator under the fuse-

US NATIONAL ARCHIVES, VIA R. L. CAVANAGH

55

lage, and there are aluminium fairings over the windings of shock-absorber cord at the apices of the V-struts of the undercarriage. The French authorities conducted performance trials of an American-built D.H.4 on 27 October 1918 and this may have been the subject aircraft.

Bearing the name *South Carolina* and with white stars painted on its wheel covers, the Liberty-Four shown in photograph 55 was an aircraft of the 85th (Observation) Aero Squadron. No. 32224 of the 50th (Observation) Aero Squadron (photograph 56) bore its squadron emblem

on the fuselage side; it also had an additional, probably personal, marking on the side of the nose. The 168th (Observation) Aero Squadron also placed its macabre emblem on the rear fuselage side. No. 32899, the subject of photograph 57, bore additionally a girl's name on the nose.

USAF MUSEUM, VIA K. M. MOLSON

56

57

D.H.4 UNITS, BASES AND MARKINGS (US)

USAS AERO

Squadron	Bases	Sqn. markings
8th (Obs)	Ourches-sur-Meuse	Silhouette of eagle with outstretched wings perched on Liberty Bell
11th (Bomb)	Delouze, Amanty, Maulan	On white disc, strip-cartoon character 'Jiggs' walking with bomb under his arm
20th (Bomb)	Amanty, Maulan	On orange disc, crouching figure with spherical bomb in each hand ('The Mad Bolshevik Bomber')
24th (Obs) (had one D.H.4 only)	Vavincourt, Gondreville-sur-Moselle	Eagle with outstretched wings pouncing on dachshund
50th (Obs)	Behonne, Picqueley	Dutch woman carrying stick raised to strike
85th (Obs)	Toul, Manonville	Winged cherub (?) wearing US Army campaign hat, seated on globe of world
91st (Obs)	Gondreville-sur-Moselle	Knight in full armour with lance couched, on galloping horse pursuing red winged devil
100th (Bomb)	Ourches-sur-Meuse	Red devil seated on falling aerial bomb
135th (Obs)	Ourches-sur-Meuse, Toul	Statue of Liberty against pattern of rays of rising sun
155th (Obs)	–	White arrowhead pointing upwards
163rd (Bomb)	Ourches-sur-Meuse	On yellow ellipse, black cat on aerial bomb
166th (Bomb)	Maulan	In white lozenge, rising sun, winged with US stars and stripes holding bomb, all behind globe of Earth
168th (Obs)	–	Winged skull in profile on black disc with white outline
278th (Obs)	Toul	On yellow disc, owl in flight holding a telescope in its talons
354th (Obs)	–	On orange disc, witch in flight on stylized skeletal aircraft with broomhead tail, on which stands black cat with telescope, looking aft

First Marine Aviation Force, Northern Bombing Group, US Naval Aviation Force[1]

Squadrons A & B[2]	Oye	
Squadrons C & D[3]	Le Fresne	See note 4 below

TRAINING UNITS

Air Instruction Centers: 1st, Paris; 2nd, Tours; 3rd, Issoudun; 7th, Clermont-Ferrand.
Aerial Gunnery School, St-Jean-des-Monts.
2nd Aero School, Châtillon.
2nd Air Observers' School, Sougé.
Air Service Production Center No. 2, Romorantin.

[1]For whch 72 D.H.4s were ordered before it left the USA: the US Army delivered a total of 155 D.H.4s to the US Navy before the war ended.
[2]Later redesignated 7th and 8th Marine Sqns.
[3]Later redesignated 9th and 10th Marine Sqns.
[4]All D.H.4s and D.H.9As used by the US Marine squadrons had, as their fuselage marking, a US roundel superimposed on an oblique anchor, surmounted by an eagle with wings spread.

DE HAVILLAND D.H.5

Role: Single-seat fighter.
Powerplant: 1 × 110hp Le Rhône 9J, 110hp Clerget 9Z or 100hp Gnome Monosoupape 9N.
Armament: One 0.303in Vickers machine gun synchronized by Constantinesco CC gear (a few aircraft may have had the Aircraft Manufacturing Co. mechanical gear); four 25lb bombs.
First flight: Autumn 1916.

Contractors	Contract nos.	Serial nos.	Qty. ordered	Qty. delivered	Remarks
Aircraft Mfg. Co.	{ 87/A/1286	A5172	1	1	
	87/A/1286	A9163–A9361	199	199	A9362 cancelled; A5172 included.
Darracq	87/A/1358	A9363–A9562	200	200	
British Caudron	87/A/1433	B331–B380	50	50	
Marsh, Jones & Cribb	87/A/1714	B4901–B5000	100	100	

In the D.H.5, Geoffrey de Havilland attempted to combine the superior performance of the tractor configuration with the unobstructed upward and forward view that the D.H.2 had given its pilot. Photograph **58** is an early portrait, taken at Hendon, of the prototype D.H.5 soon after completion. At the time it had no gun, its fuselage sides had only small flank fairings behind the engine cowling, and the rudder was small but had a balance area. The prototype flew to France on 26 October 1916, landing at No. 1 Aircraft Depot, St-Omer. Two days later it flew on to No. 2 AD, Candas, where photograph **59** was taken. By that time it had acquired a small spinner, and its serial number, A5172, had been painted on its rudder. It was still unarmed.

Piloted by Flight Sergeant M. W. Piercey, A5172 flew back to the Southern Aircraft Repair Depot at Farnborough on 16 November 1916. The next day Brigadier-General Brooke-Popham wrote to the Director of Aeronautical Equipment, requesting that a gun be fitted to the aircraft and that its mounting should be capable of elevation through 45 degrees; he also suggested that the centre-section be done away with entirely to allow rearward view. The official reply of 21 November stated that it was proposed to do away with the centre-section on the third or fourth aircraft. One assumes that the spars and cross-bracing would be retained, but confirmation that any D.H.5 was thus modified has yet to be found: certainly the production

58

59

60

aircraft that went to the squadrons had the normal, fully covered centre-section. With its gun fitted, A5172 underwent performance and handling trials at the Central Flying School on 9 December 1916 and was given a satisfactory report. By that time, as

photograph **60** shows, it had been given a larger rudder of more elegant form. It seems likely that the aircraft was modified to production standard, for it was again reported at No. 1 AD in April 1917. On 20 April it was crashed by Captain Ainslie, but it was

flying again on 30 April and was on the strength of No. 24 Squadron up to 3 June 1917 when, damaged, it was sent to No. 2 AD.

The production D.H.5 had the refinement of full-length fairings on the fuselage top and sides, and on the

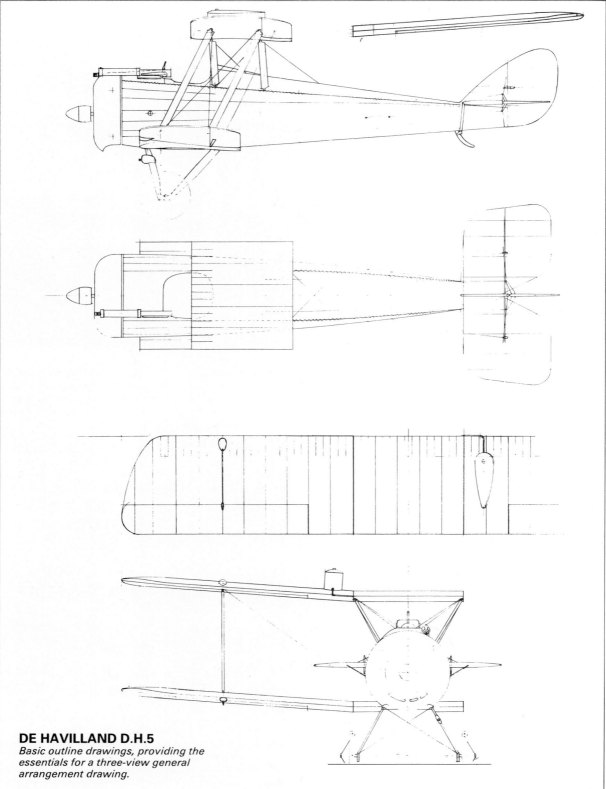

DE HAVILLAND D.H.5
*Basic outline drawings, providing the
essentials for a three-view general
arrangement drawing.*

61

early aircraft the engine cowling presented a wholly smooth external appearance, as seen in photograph **61** on A9197, a D.H.5 that was used by No. 68 Squadron RFC (later No. 2 Squadron, Australian Flying Corps) while working up at Harlaxton. That it was a presentation aircraft is obvious, though it is doubtful whether A9197 wore the inscription for long. Production of the D.H.5 was retarded

in the spring of 1917 because the French did not honour the agreed allocations of 110hp Le Rhône engines: in April and May they took the entire output of these engines (272), of which 72 should have gone to the RFC.

The inscription on the flank of A9513 (photograph **62**) reads: 'Presented by the Native Administration of Benin in Southern Provinces of

Nigeria'. This D.H.5 had the reinforced engine cowling that was introduced in the summer of 1917 and also the standard installation of a fixed Vickers gun offset to port. The elevating mounting tested on A5172 was not fitted to production D.H.5s. The Vickers was synchronized by the Constantinesco CC Fire Control Timing Gear – a fact confirmed by the hydraulic lead seen emerging through

62

the top decking to connect with the Type B trigger motor on the gun. The Constantinesco installation in the D.H.5 gave a great deal of trouble. By 12 May 1917 two squadrons were out of action owing to the failure of their CC gears. A suitable modification had been devised by 13 June 1917 but its introduction was expected to take at least three weeks. A9513 was at Hendon Aircraft Acceptance Park when it was allocated to the RFC in France on 15 October 1917. It must have been one of the last D.H.5s to be with an operational unit in the field, for it was returned to an AD from No. 32 Squadron as late as 8 March 1918, being flown back to England two days later. It was finally struck off on 5 May 1918.

The first Darracq-built D.H.5, A9363 (photograph **63**), had been delivered to the Aircraft Inspection Department at Farnborough by 25

A. E. FERKO

OPERATIONAL UNITS (RFC)

Squadron	Bases	Sqn. markings
24	Flez, Baizieux, Teteghem, Marieux	Single vertical white bar on fuselage side ahead of roundel
32	Léalvillers, Abeele, Droglandt	White band, approximately half diameter of fuselage roundel, encircling fuselage immediately abaft roundel
41	Abeele, Léalvillers	One white bar either side of roundel on fuselage
64	Le Hameau	White equilateral triangle abaft roundel on fuselage
68 (Australian)[1]	Baizieux	White band around fuselage just ahead of tailplane

SQUADRONS MOBILIZING
No. 28, Yatesbury; No. 64, Sedgeford; No. 65, Wye; No. 68, Harlaxton.

TRAINING UNITS
Training Sqns. No. 10, Shawbury; No. 40, Croydon; No. 43, Tern Hill; No. 45, South Carlton; No. 55, Yatesbury; No. 62, Dover; No. 63, Joyce Green; No. 30 (Australian),[2] Tern Hill. No. 3 Training Depot Station, Lopcombe Corner.

[1]Later No. 2 Sqn., Australian Flying Corps.
[2]Later redesignated No. 6 Training Squadron, Australian Flying Corps.

April 1917, on which date it was allocated to 'H' Replacement Squadron, which proved to be No. 24 Squadron; in it, A9363 was aircraft 'W'. It was the first D.H.5 of the squadron to shoot down an enemy aircraft: on 25 May 1917 Lt. S. Cockerell shot down and destroyed an Albatros D.III over Ligny. It was again victorious on 21 September 1917, when Lt. W. H. Strathan drove down another Albatros D.III between Anneux and Rumilly-en-Cambrésis.

A9435 was originally allocated to No. 68 Squadron on 16 August 1917, while it was still at Hendon Aircraft Acceptance Park. Evidently it went instead to No. 24 Squadron, but its operational career, as aircraft 'E' of the unit, was brief. On 10 September 1917 it was captured intact and its pilot, 2/Lt. G. P. Robertson, was made a prisoner of war. For evaluation the Germans sent A9435 to Adlershof, where photograph **64** was taken. Another captive D.H.5 was A9474 of No. 41 Squadron, seen in photograph **65** in a somewhat dilapi-

dated condition in German hands, robbed of its tyres and with its mainplanes unbraced. Its companions in misfortune are the S.E.5a B4876, which had been captured on 20 October 1917, and an unidentified Camel. A9474 was first allocated to the RFC in France on 10 September 1917 and was issued to No. 41 Squadron on 14 October. It fell into enemy hands on 29 October as aircraft 'F' of its squadron, and 2/Lt. F. S. Clark became a prisoner of war.

Prominent in any three-quarter rear

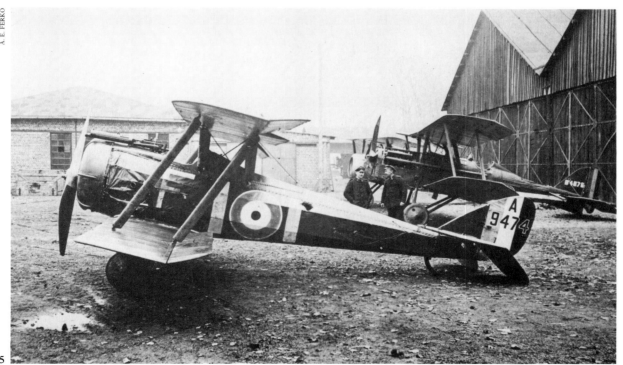

65

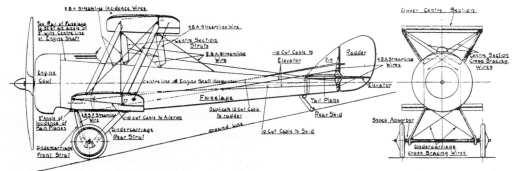

SIDE ELEVATION OF MACHINE.
Fig 1
TRUING UP

FRONT ELEVATION OF CENTRE SECTION
Fig 2
TRUING UP

Flying Position.

To get Machine in flying position, level transversely and adjust longitudinally until the incidence of the Lower Centre Planes is 2°. Check by Straightedge and Abney level.

Truing up Fuselage.

Tension all Internal Cross Bracing Wires until corresponding diagonals are equal throughout. By means of Top Cross Bracing wires, true up until all mid points of Top Cross Struts are in one Straight line. By means of Side Cross Bracing wires (on one side) true up until mid points of Struts of Rear portion on that side, are in line, and a point 4" below mid point of Front Strut is in the same line. Place a Straightedge (winding board) across the Top Longerons just in front of second bay from the Tail. By means of the Side Cross Bracing Wires on the other side true up until the upper edge of another Straightedge placed transversely across the Top Longerons at any point, is in line with the Upper edge of the first Straightedge. Tension the Bottom Cross Bracing Wires.

Undercarriage.

True up undercarriage by adjusting Front Cross Bracing Wires until corresponding diagonals are equal. Check by trammel.

Centre Section.

True up by means of Centre Section Diagonal Bracing Wires. True up until Centre Section is symmetrical about Vertical Centre Line of machine and Check by trammel. By means of the Side Bracing Wires true up until the Stagger is as shown in Fig 4 and the Incidence of Upper & Lower Centre Section Planes is 2° Check as shown in Fig 4.

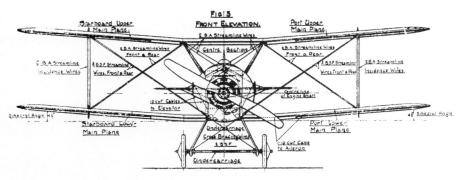

Fig 3
FRONT ELEVATION.

MAIN PLANES

Dihedral:-

The dihedral angle is 4½° for both Upper & Lower Main Planes. Check by straightedge along Spars & Abney Level. A line stretched over Upper Main Planes from tops of Front Outer Struts should be 5¾" vertically above Upper Centre Section Plane.

Incidence.

2° throughout in Starboard Main Planes, 2° at root of the Port Main Planes and 2½° at Outer Strut of the Port Main Planes on account of Propeller Torque. Check by Straightedge & Abney level.

Stagger.

(See Fig 4) Check for Uniformity by holding Straightedges from Leading Edge of Upper Main Planes to Leading Edge of Lower Main Planes and Aligning them.

Ailerons.

The droop of the Ailerons is ⅜" with Pilots Control Stick Central.

POSITION OF UPPER MAIN PLANES
IN RELATION TO LOWER MAIN PLANES

FIG 4.

Drop plumb line from a point 2" behind centre of Top Front Spar and strike a point 2¾" behind Centre of Bottom Rear Spar with Lower Centre Section Planes at 2° Incidence.

DE HAVILLAND D.H.5
Official rigging diagrams (continued opposite).

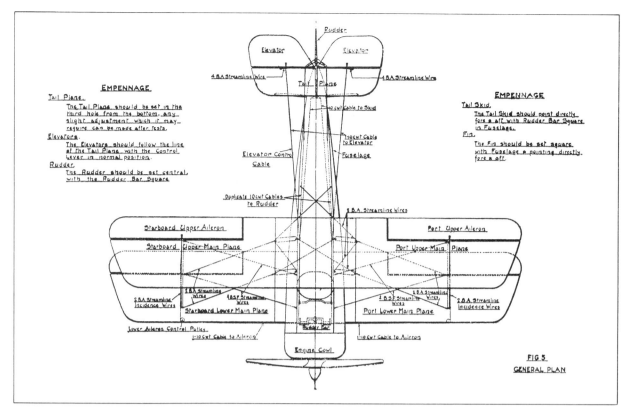

EMPENNAGE

Tail Plane.
The Tail Plane should be set in the third hole from the bottom, any slight adjustment which it may require can be made after tests.

Elevators.
The Elevators should follow the line of the Tail Plane with the Control Lever in normal position.

Rudder.
The Rudder should be set central, with the Rudder Bar Square

EMPENNAGE

Tail Skid.
The Tail Skid should point directly fore & aft with Rudder Bar Square in Fuselage.

Fin.
The Fin should be set square with Fuselage & pointing directly fore & aft.

FIG 5
GENERAL PLAN

view of a D.H.5 is the overwing gravity tank (capacity 5 gallons) on the starboard upper mainplane. The Darracq-built aircraft depicted in photograph **66**, A9507, was at Hendon Aircraft Acceptance Park on 10 October 1917. It went to No. 64 Squadron, acquiring the status of a presentation aircraft and with it the fuselage inscription 'Christchurch Over Seas Club'. A9507's pilot adapted his aircraft's identity letter to ensure that it recorded the name *Elsa*, presumably that of a girlfriend, fiancée or female relative. This D.H.5 survived the war, even if only briefly:

it was flown back to England on 15 February 1918 and was reported to be still in store at Southport on 18 January 1919.

No. 68 Squadron RFC was an Australian unit, and in January 1918 it took up a new identity as No. 2 Squadron Australian Flying Corps.

66

67

68

That occurred at the time when it relinquished its D.H.5s on re-equipping with S.E.5as. D.H.5 A9288 (photograph 67) was used by No. 68 Squadron, and here wears the unit's marking of a narrow white band round the rear fuselage. After its withdrawal from operations A9288 was flown back to England on 15 February 1918.

The D.H.5 suffered from severe vibration that proved difficult to rectify; early deliveries of the type were delayed while a remedy was sought. The engine bearer plate was redesigned, apparently bringing about some improvement. Whether this problem created secondary difficulties with the engine cowling is not entirely clear: apart from the addition of the stiffening ribs mentioned against photograph 60, the well-cambered and full-circular cowling remained standard. Nevertheless, in May 1917 No. 65 Squadron (which had some D.H.5s during its working-up period) reported that it had greatly reduced vibration on its aircraft by cutting away the cowling. A9377, the subject of photograph 68, had its cowling cut away to make it of horse-shoe form, but it is not known whether this had been inspired by No. 65 Squadron's experiences or had merely been done in the interests of engine cooling, for A9377 existed only in the summer months of 1917. On 31 May 1917, while under allocation to Training Brigade, it was reallocated to the Expeditionary Force. Next day this was reversed, and the aircraft was allocated to Training Brigade. It was with No. 40 Training Squadron, Croydon, for a time but moved on to No. 62 Training Squadron at Dover. While with the latter unit A9377 crashed on 25 September 1917; its unfortunate pilot, 2/Lt. H. M. Lee, lost his life.

A D.H.5 that should have been preserved was A9340. In 1918 a large and varied selection of contemporary aircraft was progressively gathered together, mostly at the Agricultural Hall, Islington, to form a museum collection for posterity. The chosen D.H.5 was A9340, which was considered to have been delivered for preservation on 23 March 1918, though it was reported to be in store at Ascot on 26 March. It has just been lent to the YWCA for that organization's Blue Triangle Week, and had been exhibited in Trafalgar Square, London, where photograph 69 taken. It was reported to have the 110hp Le Rhône engine No. 35563/W.D.101089. First allocated to the Expeditionary Force on 24 October 1917, A9340 had seen service with No. 32 Squadron, whose markings it still bore when photographed. It was returned to an Aircraft Depot from the squadron on 5 March 1918 and was flown back to England on 15 March. It must have been taken to Trafalgar Square almost immediately after its arrival in England. It did not, alas, survive: of all the many historic aircraft delivered for preservation, only one, the Short 184 that flew at Jutland, remained after the mindless destruction of all the others in the early 1920s.

DE HAVILLAND D.H.6

Role: Two-seat trainer and coastal patrol/anti-submarine aircraft.
Powerplant: 1 × 90hp RAF 1a, 90hp Curtiss OX-5 or 80hp Renault.
Armament: A Lewis machine gun could be mounted on the rear cockpit. Bomb load of about 100lb on anti-submarine aircraft.
First flight: Early 1917.

Contractors	Contract nos.	Serial nos.	Qty. ordered	Qty. delivered	Remarks
Aircraft Mfg. Co.	87/A/910	A5175–A5176	2	2	
Grahame-White	87/A/1359	A9563–A9762	200	200	15 to RNAS.
Aircraft Mfg. Co.	87/A/1844	B2601–B3100	500	500	81 to RNAS.
	A.S.17567	B9031–B9130	100	4	96 cancelled.
Grahame-White	87/A/1359	C1951–C2150	200	200	18 to RNAS.
Kingsbury	A.S.22909	C5126–C5275	150	150	2 to RNAS.
Harland & Wolff	A.S.19062	C5451–C5750	300	100	200 cancelled 28 March 1918.
Morgan	A.S.20465	C6501–C6700	200	200	4 to RNAS.
Savages	A.S.19896	C6801–C6900	100	100	
Ransomes, Sims & Jeffries	A.S.18918	C7201–C7600	400	250	150 cancelled.
Grahame-White	87/A/1359	C7601–C7900	300	300	At least 37 to RNAS.
Gloucester	A.S.32956	C9336–C9485	150	150	
Grahame-White	A.S.32667	D951–D1000	50	50	To Egypt in components.
Aircraft Mfg. Co	87/A/1844	D8581–D8780	200	–	Cancelled.
	35a/1050/C.1391	F3346–F3441	96	96	
Canadian Aeroplanes			1	1	

The D.H.6 was designed to be easy to produce and easy to fly, for it was conceived purely as a trainer. Its structural simplicity should have been a production asset – especially at a time when the expansion of the RFC demanded a corresponding increase in the number of trained pilots – but faulty timber not only delayed production but also led to fatal crashes.

The first prototype (photograph **70**) had the elegant de Havilland fin and rudder, and its fuselage had a rounded top decking; its mainplanes were uncompromisingly angular, and

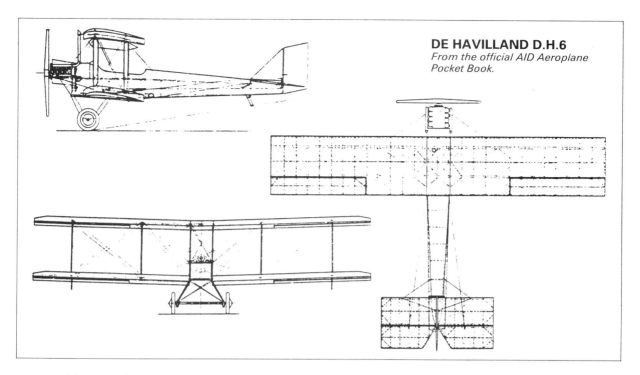

DE HAVILLAND D.H.6
From the official AID Aeroplane Pocket Book.

upper and lower surfaces were interchangeable. Production on a large and growing scale was ordered.

Production D.H.6s were even more angular than the prototypes. The fin and rudder were redesigned to have wholly rectilineal profiles, and the rear top decking of the fuselage was similarly squared off. On the early production aircraft the 90hp RAF 1a remained the standard engine. Typical of such D.H.6s was A9580 (photograph **71**), which is known to have been used by No. 16 Training Squadron, Beaulieu, in 1917. The

71

CHAZ BOWYER

72

D.H.6 UNITS, BASES AND MARKINGS

COASTAL PATROL UNITS[1]

Squadrons	Flights	Bases[2]
236	515, 516	Mullion
241	513	Chickerill
242	514	Telscombe Cliffs
244	521, 522	Bangor
	530	Dublin
248	404	North Coates Fitties
250	500, 501	Padstow
251	504	Atwick
	505, 510	West Ayton
	506	Owthorne
252	507, 508	Tynemouth
	509	Seaton Carew
253	511, 512	New Bembridge
254	517, 518	Prawle Point
255	519, 520	Pembroke (Tenby)
256	525	Ashington
	526	New Haggerston
	527, 528	Seahouses
258	523, 524, 529	Luce Bay
260	502, 503	Westward Ho!
272	531, 532, 533	Machrihanish

TRAINING SQUADRONS (RFC/RAF)

No. 4, Northolt; No. 7, Netheravon, Witney; No. 8, Witney; No. 11, Scampton; No. 13, Yatesbury; No. 15, Doncaster, Spittlegate; No. 16, Beaulieu, Yatesbury; No. 17, Croydon, Oxford, Yatesbury; No. 20, Wyton, Spittlegate, Harlaxton; No. 21, Ismailia; No. 23, Abu Qir; No. 24, Netheravon, Wyton; No. 25, Thetford; No. 29 (Australian), Shawbury, Minchinhampton; No. 31, Wyton; No. 32 (Australian), Yatesbury, Leighterton; No. 35, Port Meadow; No. 39, Montrose, South Carlton; No. 42, Hounslow, Wye; No. 44, Harlaxton, Waddington; No. 46, Bramham Moor, Catterick; No. 48, Waddington; No. 50, Narborough, Spittlegate; No. 51, Waddington; No. 52, Montrose, Catterick; No. 53, Narborough, Harlaxton; No. 54, Harlaxton, Castle Bromwich, Eastbourne; No. 59, Yatesbury, Beaulieu, Netheravon, Lilbourne, Rendcombe; No. 61, South Carlton; No. 64, Narborough, Harlaxton; No. 66, Yatesbury; No. 68, Bramham Moor; No. 69, Narborough; No. 190, Rochford, Newmarket;

No. 191, Marham; Nos. 193 and 194, Amria; No. 200 Night Trg. Sqn., East Retford. No. 5 Australian FC, Shawbury; No. 7 Australian FC, Yatesbury, Leighterton. Camp Leaside, North Toronto, Ontario, Canada.

TRAINING STATIONS (RNAS)

Chingford, Cranwell (including Gunnery School at Frieston), Eastbourne, Eastchurch, Manstone, Redcar. Aegean area: Mudros, 'F' Squadron.

TRAINING DEPOT STATIONS

No. 1, Stamford; No. 3, Lopcombe Corner; No. 5, Easton-on-the-Hill; No. 8, Netheravon; No. 9, Shawbury; No. 10, Harling Road; No. 11, Old Sarum; No. 12, Netheravon; No. 16, Amria; No. 20, Amria, Shallufa; No. 21, Driffield; No. 31, Fowlmere; No. 35, Thetford; No. 37, Yatesbury; No. 40, Harlaxton; No. 48, Waddington; No. 49, Catterick; No. 50, Eastbourne; No. 57, Cranwell; No. 203, Manstone; No. 204, Eastchurch; No. 211, Huntingdon.

SQUADRONS MOBILIZING

No. 61, Rochford; No. 64, Sedgeford; No. 66, Filton; No. 68, Harlaxton; No. 69, Narborough; No. 76, Copmanthorpe; No. 77, Turnhouse; No. 97, Netheravon; No. 103, Old Sarum; No. 105, Ireland; No. 110, Sedgeford; No. 121, Narborough; No. 131, Shawbury.

OTHER TRAINING UNITS

Schools of Navigation & Bomb Dropping: No. 1, Stonehenge; No. 2, Andover; No. 3, Helwan.
No. 3 School of Aerial Gunnery, Driffield.
School of Aerial Gunnery, Abu Qir.
Marine Observers' Schools: No. 1, Aldeburgh; No. 2, Eastchurch.
No. 2 Wireless School, Penshurst.
Artillery Observers' School, Almaza.
Australian Central Flying School, Point Cook.

---

[1]No authentic details of squadron markings of such units are known; indeed, it is doubtful whether any such markings were ever authorized for any of the coastal squadrons.
[2]Ten D.H.6s went to US Naval Aviation for coastal patrol duties from unspecified bases in the British Isles.

three-quarter rear view of C6833 (photograph 72) emphasizes the dimensions of the original production-type rudder and elevators. So great was the chord of the latter that they almost touched the ground when the aircraft was at rest. C6833 was at some time a D.H.6 of No. 10 Training Depot Station, Harling Road, but it cannot be stated with certainty that the twin white bands on its fuselage were the marking of that unit or of one of its constituent Training Squadrons. The root rib-space behind the rear spar of the starboard lower wing has had its fabric removed, presumably to improve the view of the ground for the occupant of the rear cockpit.

Although the D.H.6 was initially believed to be viceless and docile to a fault, it was found that, in aerobatic flying, difficulty was experienced in pulling out from dives at more than 100mph. This phenomenon was investigated progressively at Farnborough: combinations of a reduction in chord of mainplanes, rudder and elevators, the adoption of negative stagger, and a marked increase in tailplane incidence were tried. Cutting four inches off the leading edges of the mainplanes markedly reduced the aerofoil's undercamber; the mainplanes were rigged with a negative stagger of 10.2 inches; and the chord of the elevators was reduced by 12 inches. One of the D.H.6s used in these trials was B2840, seen in photograph 73 with all the flight-surface modifications visible. At one stage this aircraft was rigged with 13½ inches of negative stagger. Introducing these modifications caused many delays in production. Although aircraft that had all the changes incorporated were designated D.H.6A, that name found little or no use in official records.

Although the D.H.6 was one of the least warlike aeroplanes in the RAF's establishment, it was pressed into operational service from the spring of 1918 as an inshore patrol and anti-submarine aircraft, and, although its weapon load was only about 100lb of bombs (sometimes only a single 100pdr), these patrols proved remarkably effective. Historically, they set a precedent for the similar use in the Second World War of the D.H.6's descendant, the Tiger Moth.

The locations of the D.H.6 Flights are set out in the accompanying table. D.H.6 C7863 (photograph 74) was an aircraft of No. 530 Flight based near Dublin. When photographed it had its fin, tailplane and elevators painted white, possibly to make the aircraft more visible if it had to come down on the sea. Many of the coastal patrol D.H.6s had the 90hp Curtiss OX-5 engine. One such was C5194 of No. 250 Squadron (Flights Nos. 500 and 501), normally based at Padstow; it is seen in photograph 75 with its rear top decking undergoing repair or

73

74

modification. The origin and significance of its fuselage marking are unknown. In the background are two Short 184 seaplanes.

With long oversea patrols being flown by the anti-submarine D.H.6s, RAF Grain was officially asked on 6 April 1918 to design suitable emergency flotation gear for the type. Several D.H.6s were sent to Grain for the necessary development work; of these, B2903 and B2929 had the

Curtiss engine. B2903 is seen in photograph **76** at Grain on 19 October 1918, with a direct-reading air-speed indicator on its port outer interplane struts: it was the subject aircraft of Test Report No. N.M.239 (see Appendix A) at which time it had no flotation gear. Although it had the reduced-chord mainplanes, it retained the original elevators. Because upper and lower wings were interchangeable, roundels were painted on the

upper and under surfaces of all mainplane panels. B2903 was at one time on the strength of No. 255 Squadron, fitted with flotation gear. B2929, also Curtiss-powered, was contemporary at Grain with B2903, sharing with it the testing recorded in Report No. N.M.239. However, at that time B2929 was fitted with Grain flotation gear, seen stowed in photograph **77**, dated 21 October 1918. The installation of the Curtiss engine did noth-

77

ing to improve the appearance of the D.H.6.

Photograph **78** shows the installation of stowed flotation gear on C2098, one of the first D.H.6s to be allocated to Grain for experimental work. Officially allocated on 31 December 1917, this aircraft was still at Hendon on 5 January 1918. It had the RAF 1a engine, driving one of the types of two-blade propellers that were later used with that engine. The

78

79

COLIN OWERS

80

photograph is dated 14 June 1918. Also taken that day was photograph **79**, showing C2098 under tow after a successful ditching; the inflated air bags can be seen. An official requisition for 200 sets of D.H.6 flotation gear had been submitted on 26 May 1918. It was later decided that the coastal D.H.6s and F.E.2bs would be replaced by D.H.9s, D.H.9As and Vickers Vimys, but relatively few D.H.9s had reached the Flights by November 1918.

Eight D.H.6s were ordered for the Australian Central Flying School at Point Cook on 20 March 1918. Those dispatched included B2801–B2804 and C9372–C9374. The original eight were sent in four different ships between June and August 1918; two lost en route in the SS *Baranga* were later replaced. Those known to have been used at Point Cook include B2802, B2803, C9372 and C9373; photograph **80**, of C9373, was taken there.

Much flying training for the RFC was carried out in Canada and the USA in 1917–18, and large-scale production of the Curtiss JN-4(Can) development of the JN-3 was undertaken by Canadian Aeroplanes Ltd. of Toronto. Perhaps as a form of insurance against the possible failure of the JN-4(Can), the D.H.6 was considered for production in Canada, and the single prototype (photograph **81**) was built by Canadian Aeroplanes. It had a 90hp Curtiss OX-5 engine, and

81

its control system was modified to be essentially similar to that of the Curtiss JN-3. Brigadier-General C. G. Hoare, who was Officer Commanding the RFC in Canada, took a direct personal interest in its making and tested it himself. With the adoption of the JN-4(Can), no D.H.6 production followed, but the prototype went to Leaside. There, according to one reminiscence, 'It was used exclusively for higher officers to put in flying time to enable them to draw flying pay'.

DE HAVILLAND D.H.7

The D.H.7 was a design for a single-seat fighter; it would have been a tractor biplane powered by either a 200hp BHP or a 190hp Rolls-Royce (Falcon) engine. It was officially reported on 9 May 1917 that general-arrangement drawings and technical data would be received during the following week. Presumably they were, and were favourably regarded, for on 17 May British Requisition No. 70 called for an order for six prototypes to be built by the Aircraft Manufacturing Co.

A contract for these prototypes (No. A.S.12985) was given on 20 May, but it is doubtful whether any work on the aircraft was started. This is perhaps not surprising: production of the BHP engine was proving troublesome, and it was needed for a substantial proportion of the D.H.4s then in production and, later and more extensively, for the D.H.9; while the Rolls-Royce engine was the standard power unit of the Bristol Fighter. Moreover, the Aircraft Manufacturing Co. was overloaded with production contracts.

As late as 4 December 1917, at the 241st Meeting of the Progress & Allocation Committee, the question was raised as to 'whether the Aircraft Manufacturing Co. were to proceed with the order of 29th [sic] May for six D.H.7 machines'. At the next meeting of the Committee, on 5 December 1917, it was decided that the order should be cancelled.

DE HAVILLAND D.H.8

Also reported on 9 May 1917 as being in course of design was the D.H.8, intended to be a 'high-performance gun machine'. It was to be a single-seat pusher armed with an unspecified 1½pdr gun, and an official report observed that 'This machine might prove very useful for the new Coventry Ordnance gun'. That weapon was still experimental in the spring of 1917, and the later installations in three D.H.4s were also experimental (see pp.36–37). As far as is known, the D.H.8 design was not developed, and no construction contract was proposed.

DE HAVILLAND D.H.9

Role: Two-seat bomber-reconnaissance aircraft.
Powerplant: 1 × 230hp Siddeley Puma, 290hp Siddeley Puma (high-compression), 230hp Galloway Adriatic or 260hp Fiat A-12; (experimental) 1 × 430hp Napier Lion (C6078), 200hp RAF 3a (F6205).
Armament: One 0.303in Vickers machine gun synchronized by Constantinesco CC gear; one 0.303in Lewis machine gun on Scarff ring mounting on rear cockpit; bomb load of two 230lb or four 112lb bombs, or equivalent weight.
First flight: August 1917.

Contractors	Contract nos.	Serial nos.	Qty. ordered	Qty. delivered	Remarks
Aircraft Mfg. Co.	A.S.17569	A7559	1	1	
Westland	A.S.17570/1/17	B7581–B7680	100	100	27 to RNAS. B7664 modified to D.H.9A under Ctt. A.S.14119/18.
Vulcan	87/A/1413	B9331–B9430	100	100	
Weir	A.S.17570	C1151–C1450	300	300	
Berwick	87/A/1185	C2151–C2230	80	80	
Aircraft Mfg. Co.	A.S.17569	C6051–C6350	300	298	C6122 and C6350 became D.H.9A prototypes.
Cubitt	A.S.26928	D451–D950	500	246	50 cancelled January 1919; remainder cancelled under War Break Clause.
NAF 2	A.S.32754	D1001–D1500	500	444	50 cancelled 26 March 1919; remainder cancelled under War Break Clause.
Mann, Egerton	A.S.17994	D1651–D1750	100	100	
Short Bros.	A.S.34886	D2776–D2875	100	100	
Aircraft Mfg. Co.	A.S.17569	D2876–D3275	400	400	
Weir	A.S.17570	D4011–D4210	200	–	Cancelled; number re-allotted for Pups.
Waring & Gillow (Alliance)	A.S.20391	D5551–D5850	300	300	50 made by Wells Aviation under sub-contract.
Westland		D5951–D6050	100	–	Cancelled; numbers re-allotted for S.E.5as.
Westland	A.S.42381	D7201–D7300	100	48	52 (D7215, D7216, D7251–D7300) cancelled. D7209 dismantled for spares.
Berwick	A.S.37725	D7301–D7400	100	30	70 cancelled 3 May 1918; balance delivered as spares to No. 3 Stores Depot, Milton.
Berwick	35a/1548/C.1649	D7331–D7380	50	50	Re-ordered August 1918.
Weir	A.S.41634	D9800–D9899	100	85	15 cancelled under War Break Clause.
Whitehead	A.S.2341	E601–E700	100	100	
Aircraft Mfg. Co.	A.S.17569	E5435, E5436	2	2	Replacements for C6350 and C6122.
	35a/418/C.296	E8857–E9056	200	200	
NAF 1	35a/409/C.297	F1–F300	300	–	Cancelled 14 September 1918.
Waring & Gillow (Alliance)	35a/416/C.295	F1101–F1300	200	200	
Westland	A.S.19174	F1767–F1866	100	?	No deliveries confirmed.
NAF 2		H3196–H3395	200	–	Cancelled.
Aircraft Mfg. Co.	35a/1546/C.1648	H4216–H4315	100	100	
	35a/166/C.120	H4316	1	–	Cancelled.
Berwick	35a/1548/C.1649	H4320–H4369	50	–	Cancelled.
Waring & Gillow (Alliance)	35a/2830/C.3177	H5541–H5890	350	345	
Weir	35a/2336/C.2643	H7563–H7612	50	–	Materials only. Cancelled under War Break Clause.
NAF 2	35a/2687/C.2982	H7913–H8112	200	–	Cancelled.
Aircraft Mfg. Co.	35a/2686/C.2981	H9113–H9412	300	261	

By mid-1917, demand, actual and potential, for the excellent Rolls-Royce Eagle engines far outstripped foreseeable production and the 200hp BHP had been chosen for large-scale production, while on 21 June 1917 it was officially decided to increase the operational strength of the RFC from 108 to 200 squadrons. By 23 July 1917 it was possible for the Controller of the Technical Department to lay before the Air Board drawings of a development of the D.H.4 powered by the production form of the BHP engine and with the pilot's cockpit moved aft to abut that of the observer. This new type was designated D.H.9 and was adopted by the Air Board on 27 July 1917. A prototype was created by modifying a production D.H.4, A7559, which arrived at Martlesham Heath on 5 October 1917 to undergo performance and handling trials. The results were not promising, the assessment unenthusiastic. In a Martlesham photograph (**82**), A7559 is seen with the Galloway Adriatic engine that had to be taken from a D.H.4, A7671, to replace the D.H.9's original Siddeley Puma: the latter, as if portending things to come, had failed.

Because the D.H.9 embodied so many major components from the D.H.4, production of the airframe should have been simpler than that of a wholly new type. Nevertheless, difficulties and delays occurred, and by 25 January 1918 only five D.H.9s had been delivered. The first production D.H.9, C6051 (photograph **83**), had arrived at Martlesham Heath on 6 November 1917, while that station was still working on A7559. Unfortunately, the D.H.9 got off to a bad start, for at about that time its designer, Geoffrey de Havilland himself, wrote with depressing candour to Trenchard, warning him that the D.H.9's performance would be inferior to that of the D.H.4 – in particular, that it would be unable to fly in formation at 15,000–16,000 feet with a full bomb load. On 16 November Trenchard wrote in bitter terms

to the Director-General of Military Aeronautics (then Major-General J. M. Salmond) concerning the D.H.9's poor prospects and the potentially disastrous effect it would have on RFC bombing operations. Although Salmond conveyed Trenchard's representations to the Air Board urgently, the die had been cast and the RFC had only a stark choice – the Puma-powered D.H.9 or nothing. C6051 arrived at No. 1 Aeroplane Supply Depot in France on 21 December 1917 and the next day was initially issued to No. 27 Squadron for appraisal. It may have gone to other

units also, for it did not return to No. 2 ASD until 28 February 1918, by which date its flying time totalled 58 hours 40 minutes. It was again flown to No. 27 Squadron on 8 March 1918.

The choice of the BHP engine for mass production had been made in January 1917; the decision to adopt the D.H.9 came six months later, by which time serious production problems were emerging in the making of the Siddeley Puma variant of the BHP. Simple prudence called for an alternative engine to be considered: not surprisingly, consideration was

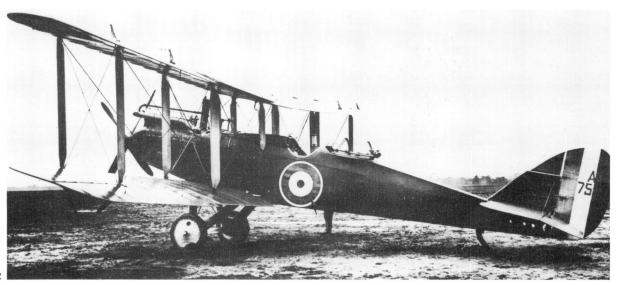

82

83

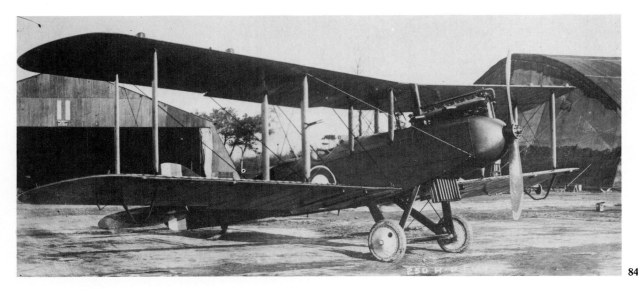

84

given to the 260hp Fiat A.12, which was similar in configuration to the BHP/Puma. It could be identified by its exhaust on the starboard side, as shown in photograph **84.** The allocation of a Fiat to the Aircraft Manufacturing Co. for the D.H.9 was first requested on 17 September 1917. By 2 November it was recorded that Westland were to make the installation and were urgently pressing for delivery of the necessary drawings and a specimen engine. On 8 November it was agreed that the RNAS should send an engine to Westlands, while on 13 November another request for a Fiat to be allocated to the Aircraft Manufacturing Co. was made. By 19 November it had been decided that Short Brothers would fit the Fiat in the batch of D.H.9s (D2776–D2875) ordered from them, but the Short aircraft had Pumas when built, in accordance with an official decision to fit the Puma that had obviously been reached by 5 February 1918. What is positively known is that a Fiat engine was installed by the Aircraft Manufacturing Co. in C6052, the second production D.H.9. This aircraft went to the Armament Experimental Station at Orfordness on 4 January 1918, whence it moved to Martlesham Heath for trials on 8 January. It returned to Orfordness on 12 February and was used there for experimental purposes; at one time it was used in tests of the Static Head Turn Indicator. Other D.H.9s known to have had the Fiat engine were C1393 and D5748.

85

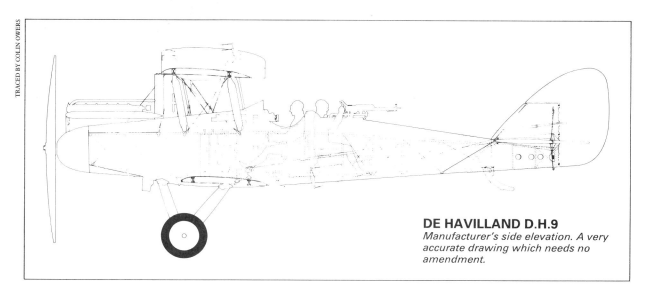

DE HAVILLAND D.H.9
Manufacturer's side elevation. A very accurate drawing which needs no amendment.

B9395 (photograph **85**) was a presentation aircraft, built by the Vulcan Motor & Engineering Co. Ltd.: 'Australia No. 28, Queensland No. 3, "The Mackenzie Tooloombah"'. It was used by No. 49 Squadron RAF and survived the war, being still on official charge on 18 January 1919.

With the Puma engine the D.H.9 was underpowered for bombing missions; moreover, the engine itself was a source of trouble and failures were not uncommon. Nevertheless, there were pilots who preferred the D.H.9 to the D.H.4 (probably because they were lucky enough to have aircraft with good examples of the Puma), especially when combat had to be joined with enemy fighters since co-operation between pilot and observer was much improved by the bringing together of their cockpits. It seems likely that engine failure was the reason why D2931 of No. 104 Squadron fell into German hands intact on 12 August 1918, when 2/Lt. O. F. Meyer and Sgt. A. C. Wallace were obliged to land at Bühl. Their aircraft bore a small white rectangular marking on each side of the fuselage (photograph **86**), but this is unlikely to have been a squadron device at that late date. When compelled to come down, Meyer and Wallace were evidently still short of their target because their D.H.9 still had its 230lb bomb on the underfuselage rack.

The RAF 3a engine did not enjoy a good reputation in the RFC, especially in No. 18 Squadron, which had D.H.4s powered by it. Perhaps

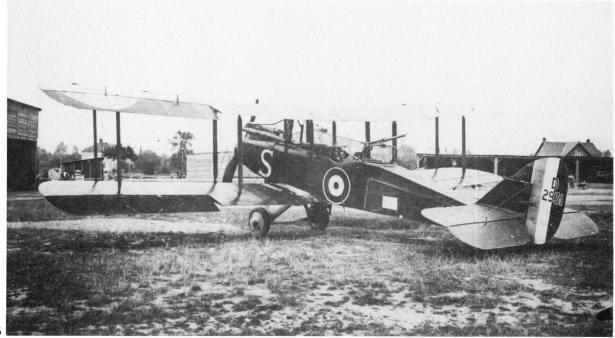

86

65

the engine's performance improved with experience, possibly to a level where it was regarded as better than the Puma, for on 5 August 1918 Brigadier-General Brooke-Popham asked No. 2 Aeroplane Supply Depot to report on the feasibility of installing an RAF 3a in a D.H.9. Such an installation was made at No. 2 ASD in F6205, a rebuilt aircraft, and was tested on 20 November 1918 by Lt. M. W. Piercey. The D.H.9 climbed to 4,000 feet in 5 minutes 20 seconds, to 10,000 feet in 16 minutes, and to 13,000 feet in 24 minutes. There the test ended: in Piercey's words, 'At 13,000 feet engine fell to pieces'. Perhaps the RAF 3a had not, after all, improved; but by the time of the test it no longer mattered.

In the heat of the Middle East No. 144 Squadron operated D.H.9s. That depicted in photograph 87, believed to be C6293, had unusual fuselage markings, but these are unlikely to have represented a squadron marking in the normal sense of the term. In the same theatre of war, Bristol Fighters of No. 67 Squadron had similar markings.

Beyond the Armistice of November 1918 some D.H.9s continued to fly operationally in the campaign against the Bolsheviks. One of those used by the RAF contingent with the North Russia Expeditionary Force was F1210, seen in photograph **88**, which was probably taken during the summer of 1919.

One of the eighteen D.H.9s given to Belgium in 1918 was F1201, seen in photograph **89** in Belgian markings but retaining its RAF serial number. This is a post-Armistice photograph taken at Bickendorf in 1919. Other D.H.9s known to have been allocated to Belgium were E8903, E8905, E8910, E8912, F1140, F1141, F1204, **89** F1221–F1229, F1275, F1293 and H9212.

B7609 (photograph **90**) was a Westland-built D.H.9 that, on 30 March 1918, was on the strength of the D.H.4 School at RNAS Manstone. It is not certain that the photograph was taken there, but the aircraft has the pilot's Vickers gun and an Aldis optical sight in place, which at least suggest a connection with operational training. On 30 March 1918, the strength of Manstone's D.H.4 School was eleven D.H.4s and the five D.H.9s B7606–B7610.

The initial forms of exhaust manifold on the D.H.9 were either the

short horizontal pipe with two outlets or the extended horizontal pipe with down-turned tail and single outlet. When these were used, the exhaust fumes were found to cause sickness in pilots and observers; additionally, the efflux distorted the pilots' forward and downward view. These faults were reported early in the D.H.9's service, but apparently it was not until late in 1918 that the L-shaped exhaust pipes of the form seen in photograph **91** on C6277 were introduced. Records suggest that these had their origins in No. 27 Squadron, a

unit that had earlier flown Puma-powered D.H.4s, on most of which a stack-type exhaust was standard. On 2 September 1918 it was reported to RFC Headquarters that the squadron had fitted a D.H.4-type exhaust to the D.H.9. On 20 September HQ instructed No. 1 ASD to put in hand the making of six similar exhaust manifolds (presumably there were by then no suitable D.H.4 spares still available in France), and on 10 November 1918 the ASD was instructed to fit five of them to D.H.9s that came in for overhaul. It is, of

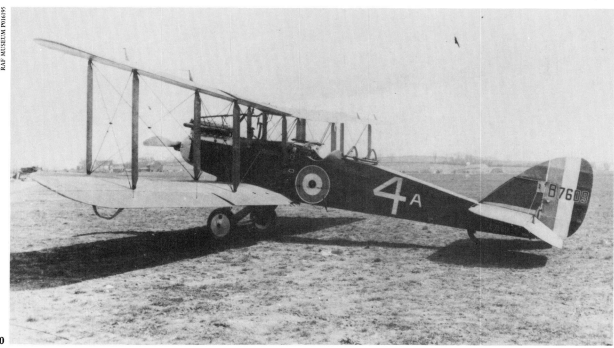

90

D.H.9 UNITS, BASES AND MARKINGS

OPERATIONAL SQUADRONS

Squadrons	Flights	Bases
17		Amberkoj, Stojakovo, Radovo, Philippopolis
27		Villers-lès-Cagnicourt, Bavay
47		Yanesh, Hajdarli, Salonika, Amberkoj, Novorossisk, Ekaterinodar, Kotelnikov, Gniloaksaiskaya, Beketovka
49		Petite-Synthe, Conteville, Fourneuil, Rozay-en-Brie, Beauvois, Villers-lès-Cagnicourt, Bavay
98		Clairmarais, Alquines, Coudekerque, Ruisseauville, Drionville, Chailly, Blangermont, Abscon, Marquain, Alquines
99		St-Omer, Tantonville, Azelot
103		Serny, Fourneuil, Serny, Floringhem, Ronchin, Maisoncelle
104		Azelot, Maisoncelle
107		Le Quesnoy-en-Artois, Drionville, Chailly, Ecoivres, Moislains, Bavay, Franc-Waret, Nivelles, Maubeuge
108		Cappelle, Bisseghem North, Gondecourt
144		Junction Station (Palestine), Haifa, Mudros, Mikra Bay, Amberkoj
202		Bergues
206[1]		Petite-Synthe, Ste-Marie-Cappel, Boisdinghem, Alquines, Boisdinghem, Alquines, Ste-Marie-Cappel, Linselles, Nivelles, Bickendorf, Maubeuge
211		Petite-Synthe, Clary, Thuillies
212	490, 557	Yarmouth
218		Petite-Synthe, Fréthun, Reumont, Vert Galant
219	555, 556	Manstone
220		Taranto, Mudros, Imbros
221	552, 553, 554	Stavros, Mudros, Baku, Petrovsk Kaskar
222		Mudros, Amberkoj, Dedeagatch
223	559, 560, 561	Mobile in Aegean area until November 1918; Mudros
224		Otranto, Andrano, Pizzone
226	472, 473, 474	Taranto, Andrano, Mudros, Taranto
233	491	Dover
236	493	Mullion
250	494	Padstow
254	492	Prawle Point
269	431, 432	Port Said
273	534	Covehithe
17th Wing	562	Malta

SQUADRONS MOBILIZING

No. 109, Lake Down; No. 110, Sedgeford; No. 117, Norwich; No. 119, Wyton; No. 120, Bracebridge Heath.

OTHER UNITS

Armament Experimental Station, Orfordness.
Wireless Experimental Establishment, Biggin Hill.

TRAINING SQUADRONS

No. 17, Shawbury; No. 25, Thetford; No. 26, Harlaxton, Narborough; No. 31, Wyton; No. 35, Port Meadow; No. 44, Waddington; No. 46, Catterick; No. 47, Waddington; No. 52, Catterick; No. 75, Cramlington.

TRAINING DEPOT STATIONS

No. 1, Stamford; No. 3, Lopcombe Corner; No. 6, Boscombe Down; No. 7, Feltwell; No. 9, Shawbury; No. 10, Harling Road; No. 11, Old Sarum; No. 14, Lake Down, Boscombe Down; No. 15, Hucknall; No. 22, Gormanston; No. 23, Baldonnel; No. 24, Collinstown; No. 25, Tallaght; No. 31, Fowlmere; No. 35, Duxford; No. 48, Waddington; No. 49, Catterick; No. 50, Eastbourne; No. 52, Cramlington; No. 57, Cranwell; No. 58, Cranwell; No. 202, Cranwell; No. 203, Manston; No. 204, Eastchurch.

RNAS TRAINING UNITS

Cranwell; D.H.4 School, Manstone.

OTHER TRAINING UNITS

Schools of Navigation & Bomb Dropping: No. 1, Stonehenge; No. 2, Andover; No. 4, Thetford.
Schools of Aerial Fighting & Gunnery: No. 1, Turnberry; No. 2, Marske; No. 3, Bircham Newton; No. 4 (Auxiliary), Marske.
No. 1 (Observers') School of Aerial Gunnery, Hythe, New Romney.
Observers' Schools: No. 1, Eastchurch; No. 2, Manstone.
Day & Night Bombing & Observers' School, Lympne.
Anti-submarine Inshore Patrol Observers' School, Aldeburgh.
Marine Observers' School, Leysdown.
School of Instruction, Southern Training Brigade, Old Sarum.
Observers' School of Reconnaissance & Aerial Photography, Shrewsbury.
School of Photography, Farnborough.

SQUADRON MARKINGS

The markings described hereunder have been attributed to Squadrons Nos. 98, 99 and 103, but the extent to which they were applied to D.H.9s of these units is uncertain. If any aircraft were so marked, their condition must have been short-lived.

No. 98 Sqn.: White zig-zag on fuselage side between roundel and tailplane.
No. 99 Sqn.: Broad white band round fuselage immediately ahead of tailplane.
No. 103 Sqn.: Two sloping white bars, one either side of fuselage roundel.
No. 144 Sqn.: At least one aircraft of this unit was marked with a long horizontal white line on the fuselage side, extending the full length of the fabric-covered portion of the rear fuselage but broken at its midpoint to permit the inclusion of the aircraft's individual number, '3'. It is uncertain whether this can be regarded as a squadron marking in the normal sense of the term.

---

[1]Earlier No. 6 (Naval) Squadron.

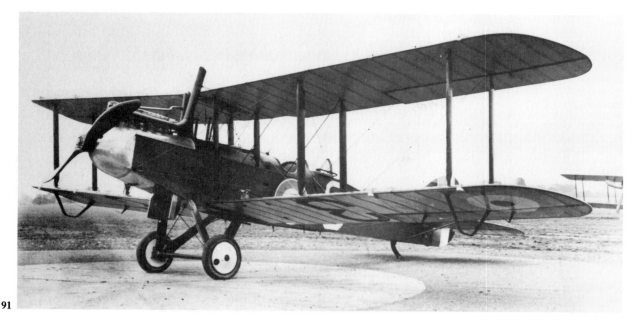

91

course, possible that the same idea occurred to other units. C6277 is believed to have been an aircraft of the Wireless Experimental Establishment, Biggin Hill. In March 1920 it was at Manstone as one of the aircraft allotted to Poland, but it did not in fact go there.

92

RAE

93

At several of the Training Depot Stations various schemes of markings were applied to the units' aircraft. Most were purely for unit identification purposes, but in some cases they tended to the exuberant, either idiosyncratically or perhaps from a functional need to be highly visible.

For whatever reason, the D.H.9 in photograph **92**, believed to be of No. 49 TDS, Catterick, had a dazzling pattern of zig-zag lines that so overshadowed its nickname *Lobster* as almost to obscure it. The aircraft at left in the photograph, wearing a US star-in-circle emblem, is D2904.

The test aircraft for the prototype Napier Lion engine was the D.H.9 C6078 and the installation was not a pretty sight (photograph **93**). It had been made at Farnborough, probably in the Southern Aircraft Repair Depot, and had been completed by 15 February 1918, when the aircraft was submitted to the AID for inspection. It made its first flight on the following day and evidently stayed at Farnborough for a considerable time: not until 12 October 1918 was it sent to Martlesham Heath for performance trials with reconnaissance and bomb loads. These extended over several months, and on its height test on 2 January 1919 Captain Andrew Lang flew it to a world record altitude of 30,500 feet. After its stay at Martlesham C6078 was returned to Airco early in February 1919. Another D.H.9 that had an experimental engine was E630, which had the 300hp RHA (Ricardo-Halford-Armstrong) Supercharger engine: its installation had been completed by 9 January 1919, and although E630 did a good deal of flying the engine was not developed.

DE HAVILLAND D.H.9A

Role: Two-seat bomber-reconnaissance aircraft.
Powerplant: 1 × 375hp Rolls-Royce Eagle VIII or 400hp Liberty 12.
Armament: One fixed 0.303in Vickers machine gun synchronized by Constantinesco CC gear; one 0.303in Lewis machine gun on Scarff ring mounting on rear cockpit; bomb load of 660lb.
First flight: February 1918.

Contractors*	Contract nos.*	Serial nos.	Qty. ordered	Qty. delivered	Remarks
Westland	A.S.14119/18	B7664	1	1	Converted D.H.9 ordered under Contract A.S.17570, having secondary installation of Rolls-Royce Eagle.
Westland	35a/400/C.276	C6122	1	1	Converted A.M.Co.-built D.H.9 with first Liberty installation: second prototype D.H.9A.
Aircraft Mfg. Co.	35a/166/C.122	C6350	1	1	First prototype D.H.9A, converted from D.H.9 ordered under A.S.17569.
Whitehead	A.S.2341	E701–E1100	400	340	60 cancelled 19 December 1918.
Aircraft Mfg. Co.	35a/412/C.291	E8407–E8806	400	400	
Mann, Egerton	35a/413/C.292	E9657–E9756	100	100	
Vulcan	35a/414/C.293	E9857–E9956	100	100	
Westland	35a/415/C.294	F951–F1100	150	150	F963 reconstructed from salvage as F9515 by No. 5 (Eastern) ARD.
Westland	35a/573/C.472	F1603–F1652	50	50	
Berwick	35a/781/C.669	F2733–F2902	170	140	30 cancelled 13 January 1919. F2747 reconstructed as H7204 17 December 1918.
Aircraft Mg. Co.	35a/1918/C.2105	H1–H200	200	169	25 cancelled 31 December 1918.
Westland	35a/2077/C.2410	H3396–H3545	150	150	
Vulcan	35a/2084/C.2414	H3546–H3795	250	120	125 cancelled 24 January 1919.
Westland	35a/3093/C.3565	J401–J450	50	–	Cancelled 31 December 1918.
Mann, Egerton	35a/3092/C.3566	J551–J600	50	50	
Aircraft Mfg. Co.	35a/3517/C.4111	J5192–J5491	300	–	Cancelled 31 December 1918.

*Wartime contracts only.

It appears that the initiative for the installation of a Rolls-Royce Eagle engine in the D.H.9 came from the Technical Department of the Ministry of Munitions shortly before Christmas 1917. An Eagle VIII was swiftly allocated for this purpose on 22 December and was soon fitted to C6350 in an installation essentially similar to that of the D.H.4 (photograph **94**). New mainplanes of increased span and chord were fitted, but all the other major components were standard D.H.4 or D.H.9 units. The completed aircraft flew to Martlesham Heath for trials on 23 February 1918 and by 9 March had acquired the new type number D.H.9A, but by that time the adoption of the 400hp Liberty 12 engine was already foreseen.

The first ten Liberty engines were delivered to Britain in March 1918. Because the Aircraft Manufacturing

94

70

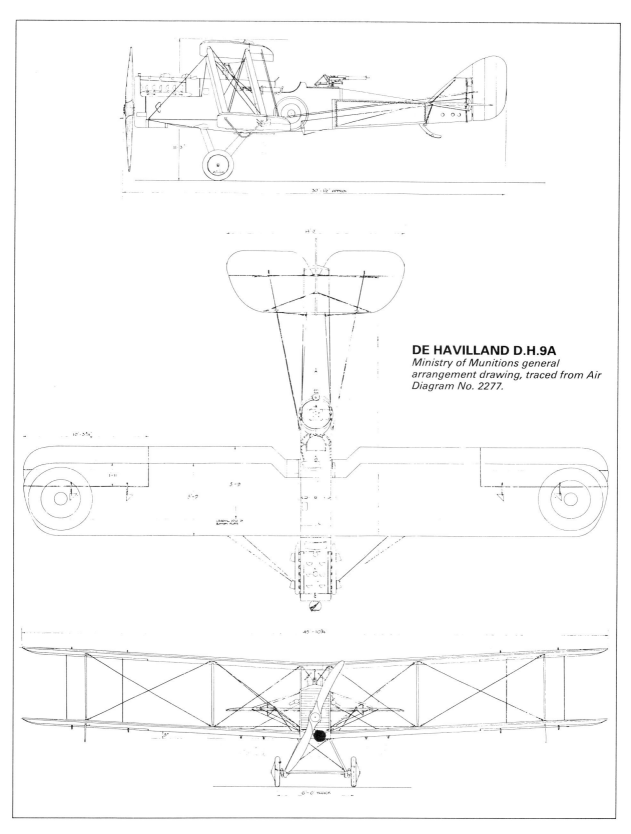

DE HAVILLAND D.H.9A
Ministry of Munitions general arrangement drawing, traced from Air Diagram No. 2277.

Company's drawing office was totally committed to work on the D.H.10, the necessary redesign of the D.H.9A to accept the American engine was undertaken by the Westland Aircraft Works. The first aircraft to have the Liberty was C6122, a converted D.H.9, which arrived at Martlesham Heath on 15 May 1918. Its trials were protracted, and on 1 August it was joined by F966, seen in photograph 95, which was the sixteenth production D.H.9A built by Westland. It, too, was exhaustively tested, and went to Orfordness on 30 August 1918. Apparently it remained there, for it was reported at Orfordness, still flying, on 8 August 1919.

Before F966 went to Martlesham the entire D.H.9A and D.H.10 programme was placed in jeopardy by the cessation of deliveries of Liberty engines in July 1918. Britain at that time had contracts for 3,000 Libertys, but America's own production programmes called for huge numbers of the engine; in particular, the US Admiralty claimed absolute priority for it (though precisely why such a claim should have been accepted is not clear). A total of 1,050 Libertys had reached Britain up to the end of July; although there was a promise of

97

750 in each of the first six months of 1919, the intervening gap came at a critical time for British aircraft production. Despite the great demands for Rolls-Royce Eagle engines for other types of aircraft, the Eagle had to be considered anew for the D.H.9A and D.H.10 – hence B7664 (photograph **96**), in which an Eagle VIII was installed in a production-type D.H.9A fuselage. This was done by Westland, and the new Eagle-9A went to Martlesham Heath on 17 August 1918. Its trials had been completed by 7 September 1918, and it went to Orfordness during the following week.

The first RAF squadron to be equipped with D.H.9As was No. 110; all of its original aircraft were presented by the Nizam of Hyderabad and were inscribed accordingly. *Hyderabad No. 7*, aircraft 'B' (photograph **97**), was F1000, a Westland-built D.H.9A: it was one of the eighteen D.H.9As that No. 110 Squadron flew to France on 31 August 1918 to join the Independent Force, RAF. Other squadrons received D.H.9As before hostilities ceased. Photograph **98** depicts F1019 as aircraft 'C' of No. 99 Squadron, with a Flight Commander's streamers on its outer rear interplane struts. It

98

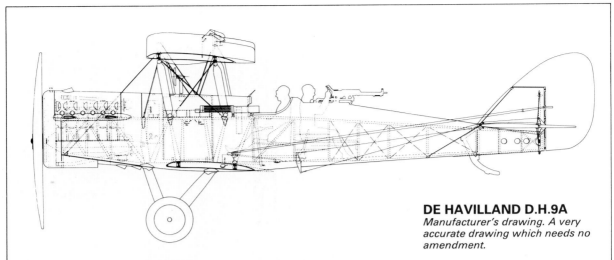

DE HAVILLAND D.H.9A
Manufacturer's drawing. A very accurate drawing which needs no amendment.

crashed at Aulnoye in December 1918. The first of No. 205 Squadron's D.H.9As came on strength in September 1918, and the squadron had been fully equipped by 1 October. In photograph **99**, taken at Verviers, F1001 is seen in the snow of February 1919.

Built by Mann, Egerton & Co. Ltd., E9665 (photograph **100**) was at one time with the Wireless Experi-

mental Establishment, Biggin Hill. On 15 February 1919 it was allocated to the Expeditionary Force, but confirmation that it went to Europe has yet to be found. One of the few Training Depot Stations known to have received D.H.9As before the war ended was No. 10 TDS, Harling Road. Among its aircraft was E9709, which was marked with a white stripe along the fuselage, surmounted by the

identifying letter 'S' (photograph **101**). This D.H.9A had been delivered to Harling Road from Norwich on 29 September 1918; it had been built by Mann, Egerton & Co. Ltd.

Like the D.H.4 and D.H.9, the D.H.9A continued to fly operationally after the Armistice in the anti-Bolshevik campaign in Russia. Photograph **102** shows the D.H.9As

99

D.H.9A UNITS AND BASES

OPERATIONAL SQUADRONS

Squadrons	Bases
18	Maisoncelle, Le Hameau, La Brayelle, Maubeuge, Bickendorf, Merheim
25	La Brayelle, Maubeuge, Bickendorf, Merheim
99	Azelot, Auxi-le-Château, St-André-aux-Bois, Aulnoye
110	Bettoncourt, Auxi-le-Château, Maisoncelle, Marquise
205	Proyart East, Moislains, Maubeuge, La Louveterie
212[1]	Yarmouth
221[2]	Petrovsk
RAF Contingent	Bereznik

SQUADRONS MOBILIZING

No. 123 (No. 2 Sqn., Canadian Air Force), Upper Heyford; No. 155, Chingford; No. 156, Wyton.

TRAINING DEPOT STATIONS

No. 7, Feltwell; No. 10, Harling Road; No. 31, Fowlmere; No. 50, Eastbourne.

OTHER TRAINING UNITS

Schools of Navigation & Bomb Dropping: No. 1, Stonehenge; No. 2, Andover; No. 4, Thetford.
Day & Night Bombing and Observers' School, Lympne.
Fleet School of Aerial Fighting & Gunnery, East Fortune.
Wireless Telephony School, Bournemouth.

US FIRST MARINE AVIATION FORCE

The RAF transferred 57 D.H.9As to the US Navy in 1918, for the use of the US Naval Northern Bomb Group: Squadrons 'A', 'B' and 'C' at Le Fresne.

[1]No. 558 Flight.
[2]Including No. 552 Flight.

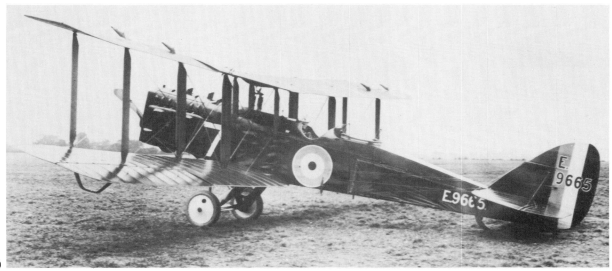

100

101

102

of No. 552 Flight (No. 221 Squadron), heavily bombed-up, awaiting the moment of take-off at Petrovsk; aircraft 'F', second from the camera, is the Westland-built F1626. After the fighting was over, abandoned D.H.9As were used by the Soviets as models for their copy of the design, the R.1, which saw quite extensive use in the Red Air Fleet. The Liberty engine was similarly copied and produced in the USSR as the M.5.

No. 2 Squadron, Canadian Air Force, was mobilizing just as the war was drawing to a close; the unit was initially formed at Upper Heyford as No. 123 (Canadian) Squadron RAF on 28 November 1918. During its very brief existence it had at least five D.H.9As, E731, E732, E8495, F1611 and F2755, of which the last-mentioned is seen in photograph **103** beside a captured Rumpler C.VII at Shoreham. The squadron had moved to Shoreham on 31 March 1919 but it was disbanded on 5 February 1920.

When the US Navy's Northern Bombing Group was formed in the summer of 1918, it was to include six US Marine squadrons, each of eighteen D.H.4s. Deliveries of US-built Liberty-Fours did not suffice to equip the squadrons; the supply of Liberty engines to the RAF ceased in July 1918, and there were engineless D.H.9As in store; but the US Marines received more Libertys than they had D.H.4 airframes. An arrangement was made that benefited both Services: for every three Marine Corps Liberty engines delivered to the RAF one was returned installed in a complete D.H.9A. By the end of the war, the Marine squadrons had between them about twenty D.H.9As and sixteen D.H.4s. The 9As retained their RAF serial numbers but were marked with US roundels, Marine Corps insignia and supplementary numbers in the E-1 to E-22 range. Photograph **104** is of E8538, which was aircraft E-15 of 'C' Squadron, First US Marine Aviation Force, and was flown by Captain J. Kendrick Noble.

103

104

DE HAVILLAND USD-9A

Role: Two-seat bomber-reconnaissance aircraft.
Powerplant: 1 × 400hp Liberty 12.
Armament: One fixed 0.3in Browning machine gun synchronized by Nelson Gun Control; two 0.3in Lewis machine guns on Scarff ring mounting on rear cockpit; normal bomb load up to 550lb (typically two 110lb and six 50lb bombs).
First flight: On or shortly before 20 July 1918.

It was intended to use the USD-9A in the US Air Service as the replacement for the Liberty-powered D.H.4 and to employ it in three capacities – as a reconnaissance aircraft, as a day bomber and as a night bomber. Initially designated USD-9, three prototypes were well advanced by early June 1918 in the workshops of the Engineering Department; additionally, experimental components of metal construction were made. In mid-July the Engineering Department's weekly Report No. 14 intimated that the USD-9 was to be redesignated USD-9A, because 'This designation is parallel to that of the English model known as the De Haviland [*sic*] 9A'. Nevertheless, the exhaustive 80-page description of the USD-9A printed in the November 1918 issue of the *Bulletin of the Experimental Department* managed to omit

totally any reference to the British origin of the design.

By 20 July 1918 the first USD-9A (presumably No. 40026) was undergoing flight tests at McCook Field, and the first of six ordered from the Dayton-Wright company was delivered to McCook on 19 August. The main airframe of the USD-9A was approved for production on 18 October 1918, and it was intended to order at least 4,000 aircraft. Continuing use of the designation USD-9, even at that late date, makes it difficult to determine precisely who was to build what, but it seems reasonable to assume that Dayton-Wright would be a contractor, as would, probably, the Curtiss Corporation, to which latter firm one of the early development USD-9As was allocated early in November 1918.

At least twelve such aircraft were

delivered, three of the earliest retaining, confusingly, the original designation USD-9. Photograph **105** depicts 40060, known as a USD-9 and here seen with its McCook Field number P-43 only partly painted on. It was being flight tested in the second week of September 1918. When photographed it had bombs on its underwing racks, and just ahead of the forward strut of the undercarriage can be seen the retractable supplementary radiator, a feature not found on the wartime British D.H.9A.

The third and fourth USD-9As (40062 and 40063) were completed early in November 1918 and were crated for dispatch overseas. Apparently they went separately, 40062 being shipped via New York on 4 November and 40063 three days later; if they ever reached Europe, their arrival seems to have gone unrecor-

105

106

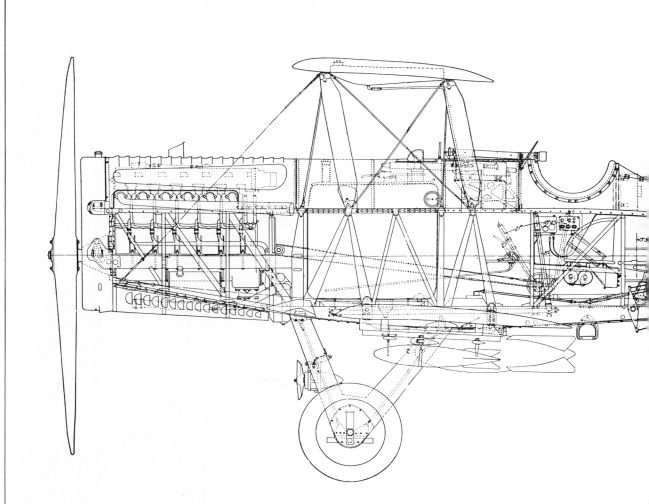

ded. As photograph **106** shows, 40062 retained the original de Havilland form of rudder, but an enlarged and more rounded rudder was designed and fitted to at least one of the USD-9As, as seen in photograph **107**. It is probable that this form of rudder would have been fitted to production aircraft.

The fuselage of the fifth USD-9A built by the Engineering Department had been used for static installation tests of armament but in mid-December 1918 it was decided to use it as the basis of the USD-9B. This variant would have been similar to the USD-9A but was to be fitted with larger wings for night bombing duties. By late December 1918 the USD-9B was reported to be 85 per cent complete.

107

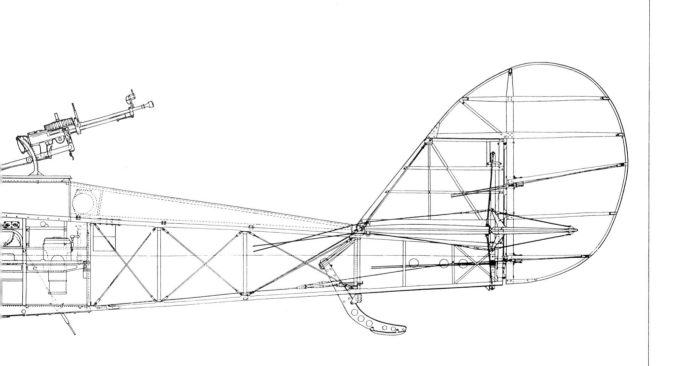

DE HAVILLAND USD-9A
Fully detailed side elevation from the Bulletin of the Experimental Department, Airplane Engineering Division, USA. It illustrates the aircraft with the later, more rounded rudder seen in photograph 107.

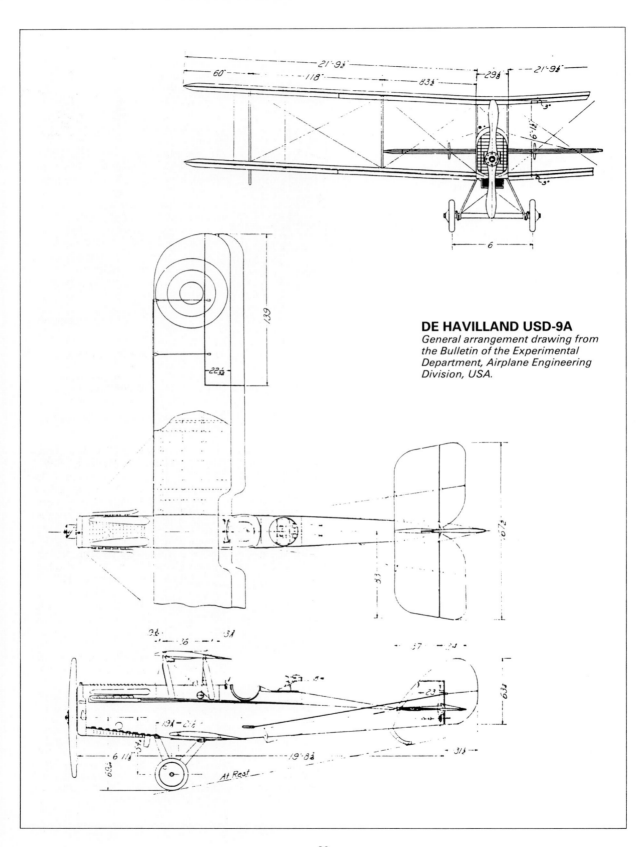

DE HAVILLAND USD-9A
General arrangement drawing from the Bulletin of the Experimental Department, Airplane Engineering Division, USA.

DE HAVILLAND D.H.10, D.H.10A AMIENS

Role: Three-seat bomber.
Powerplant: (Amiens Mk. I) 2 × 230hp Siddeley Puma; (Amiens Mk. II) 2 × 375hp Rolls-Royce Eagle VIII; (Amiens Mks. III, IIIa) 2 × 400hp Liberty 12; (Amiens Mk. IIIc) 2 × 375hp Rolls-Royce Eagle VIII.
Armament: Three to five 0.303in Lewis machine guns, one or two on Scarff ring mounting on bow cockpit, one or two on Scarff ring mounting on rear cockpit and one floor-mounted to fire aft under the tail; bomb load of up to six 230lb bombs or equivalent.
First flights: (First prototype) 4 March 1918; (second prototype) 20 April 1918; (third prototype) mid-June 1918; (fourth prototype) mid-1918.

Contractors	Contract nos.	Serial nos.	Qty. ordered	Qty. delivered	Remarks
Aircraft Mfg. Co.	{ A.S.31576	{ C8658–C8660 } { C4283 }	4	4	{ 1st–3rd prototypes. { 4th prototype.
	35a/427/C.314	E5437–E5636	200	122	E5550 and E5557 became D.H.10Cs. E5559–E5636 cancelled June 1919.
Birmingham Carriage	35a/426/C.308	E6037–E6136	100	19	80 cancelled December 1918.
Siddeley Deasy	35a/424/C.312	E7837–E7986	150	28	50 cancelled 30 January 1919; balance cancelled 13 May 1919.
Daimler	35a/432/C.313	E9057–E9206	150	40	110 cancelled November 1918.
NAF 2	35a/425/C.311	F351–F550	200	7	At least 7 delivered. 75 cancelled; further 113 cancelled 12 July 1919.
Aircraft Mfg. Co.	35a/509/C.385	F1867–F1882	16	16	F1869 was D.H.10A.
Alliance	35a/1452/C.1527	F7147–F7346	200		25 cancelled January 1919; further 150 cancelled 7 August 1919. No production recorded.
Mann, Egerton	35a/1782/C.1904	F8421–F8495	75	32	D.H.10A; F8441 was D.H.10C. Fifteen cancelled 15 December 1918; further 28 cancelled July 1919.
Aircraft Mfg. Co.	35a/2033/C.2293	H2746–H2945	200	—	40 cancelled 19 December 1918. No subsequent production recorded.

The D.H.10 was developed from the D.H.3 to meet the new mid-1917 Specification A.2.b for a day bomber. On 4 August 1917 an order was placed with the Aircraft Manufacturing Co. for three 'De Hav. 3 (designed to take B.H.P. engine)'. Clearly, if the Specification were to be met, the new aircraft would be rather more than simply a D.H.3 airframe with BHP engines, and the new design had been redesignated D.H.10 by 18 October 1917, when British Requisition No. 221 called for four experimental 'de Hav. 10' aircraft. These were ordered, in advance of the formal

Contract No. A.S.31576; their serial numbers were allocated in December, C8658–C8660 on the 18th, C4283 on the 31st. It was originally specified that the wings should fold, as on the D.H.3, to a width of less than 35 feet, but no D.H.10 had folding wings.

At about the time of the first prototype's maiden flight, the name 'Amiens' was officially allocated to the D.H.10, which thus became the first de Havilland design to be given an official name. The announcement of 6 March 1918 described the aircraft as 'Long Distance Fighter (Bombing Escort) Type de H.10 with twin 220-

hp B.H.P. engines'. The first prototype, or Amiens Mark I, C8658 (photograph **108**), made its first flight on 4 March and went to Martlesham Heath for official trials on 7 April. There it was evaluated as a bomber with crew of three and as a Home Defence fighter with crew of two. Too underpowered to meet the Specification requirements as a bomber, C8658 was sent direct to No. 51 (Home Defence) Squadron at Marham on 4 May 1918, whereafter nothing further was heard of the possible use of the D.H.10 as a Home Defence fighter.

Expansive ideas about the potential versatility of the D.H.10 were entertained. On 6 March 1918, with C8658 still undergoing makers' trials and the Eagle engines for C8659 just received by the Aircraft Manufacturing Co., the type was still primarily being considered as a long-range escort fighter, but it was recognized as likely to meet the specifications for Air Force Types VI (short-range day bomber), VIII (long-range day bomber) and XI (long-range gun machine). Although, as photograph

108

109 proves, C8659 was completed and flown, it never went to Martlesham Heath for trials. It differed significantly from C8658 in having its engines (Rolls-Royce Eagle VIII) installed as tractors, and its wings had 4 degrees of sweepback.

With Eagle engines in great demand and alarmingly few in number, it is not surprising that the Liberty engine was adopted for the D.H.10, especially in view of the yet-to-be-thwarted expectation of deliveries of 3,000 Libertys against British contracts. The third prototype, C8660, had been intended to have two Siddeley Pumas. On 4 March 1918 it was agreed to supply two Pumas for the aircraft, but obviously the poor performance of C8658 must have led to a change of mind. C8660 appeared in June with two Liberty 12 engines in nacelles with unnecessarily long fairings (photograph **110**); it had modified wing tips and horn-balanced ailerons, and it dispensed with the nose wheels that had been fitted to its two predecessors. The aircraft arrived at Martlesham on 24 June and was thoroughly tested. It crashed shortly before 3 August but was repaired and went to Orfordness on 16 August.

The evaluation process at Martlesham continued with the fourth prototype C4283 (photographs **111** and

111

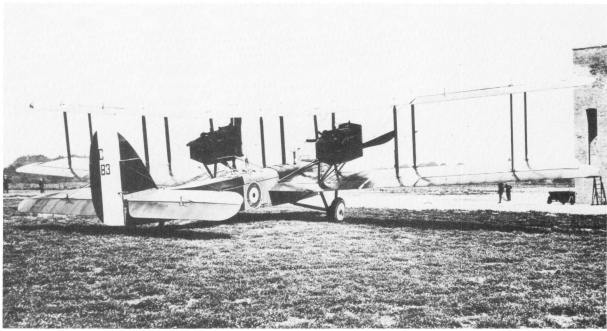

112

112), which had arrived there on 28 July 1918. This was truly the production prototype, with glazed panels in the nose to assist bomb aiming, neater engine nacelles, slightly raked wing tips and increased tailplane incidence. The engines were, of course, Liberty 12s. From Martlesham, C4283 flew direct to France on 29 August 1918 to join the Independent Force, RAF. Not until 18 September 1918 was its arrival at

No. 3 Aircraft Depot, Courban, recorded. It was briefly with No. 104 Squadron, in company with F1867. In January 1919 it was at Lympne, reallocated to the Independent Force, but this was amended on 28 January to an allocation to the South-East Area. At that time C4283 was to remain at Lympne dismantled.

The original contract for four prototypes was increased by the addition of sixteen further aircraft (F1867–

F1882), and was then assimilated into a new contract (35a/509/C.385). F1867 was flown to France on 15 September 1918 by Captain B. C. Hucks, and was in all probability the only D.H.10 to drop bombs operationally before the war ended. On 10 November, the eve of the Armistice, Captain Ewart Garland of No. 104 Squadron flew it in a raid on Sarrebourg. F1868 arrived in France on that same day. The subject of photo-

DE HAVILLAND D.H.10

Official Air Diagram for the type.

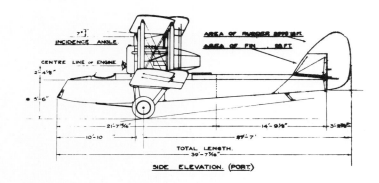

SIDE ELEVATION. (PORT)

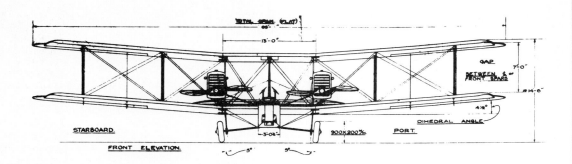

FRONT ELEVATION.

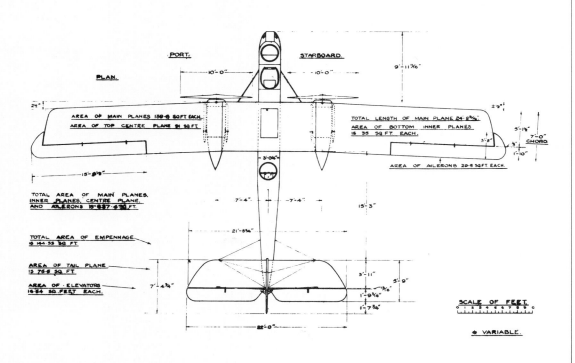

113

graph **113**, F1874, was a typical production D.H.10; though too late to see operational use, it arrived at the RAE, Farnborough, from Shotwick on 22 October 1919. F351 (photograph **114**) was the first D.H.10 to be completed by National Aircraft

Factory No. 2 at Heaton Chapel, Stockport. It was probably completed in the third week of February 1919, and its career was brief: it crashed, and it is unlikely that it was repaired.

All known photographs of D.H.10s in squadron service date from the

post-Armistice period. The type's service – almost entirely in the Middle East and India – was not without its perils: accidents occurred immediately after take-off and on landing approaches, and the type acquired a reputation for being dangerous.

114

DE HAVILLAND D.H.10A
Manufacturer's general arrangement drawing.

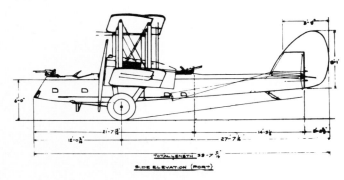

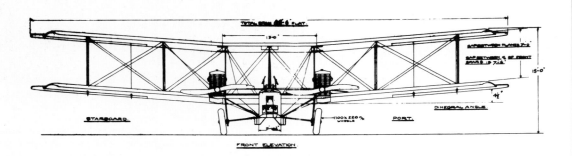

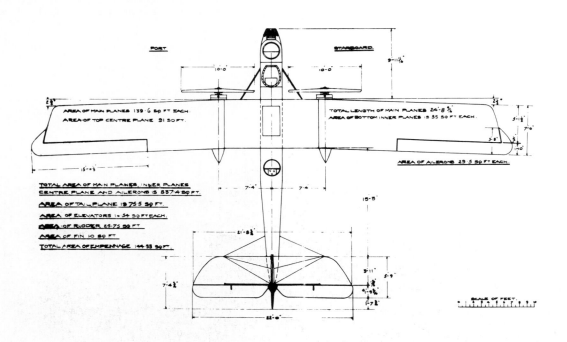

These mishaps were caused by the failure of one engine. The tachometers were mounted on the engines, not on the pilot's instrument panel, and thus they were behind and to either side of the pilot and a swing caused by engine failure could pass the danger point before a pilot realized that one of his engines had lost power. Photograph **115** is of a D.H.10 of No. 216 Squadron, probably taken in 1920 at Abu Sueir, before the enlarged radiators were introduced on D.H.10s based in the Middle East.

In the D.H.10A the engines were mounted directly on the lower wings, the first such installation being made on F1869, seen in photograph **116**. It arrived at Martlesham Heath on 17 August 1918 and, as the subject of Trials Report No. M.225a, earned a generally favourable assessment, showing a distinct improvement over the performance of C4283, the fourth prototype. F1869 left Martlesham on 15 September, bound for Hendon and Paris. It underwent further perform-

115

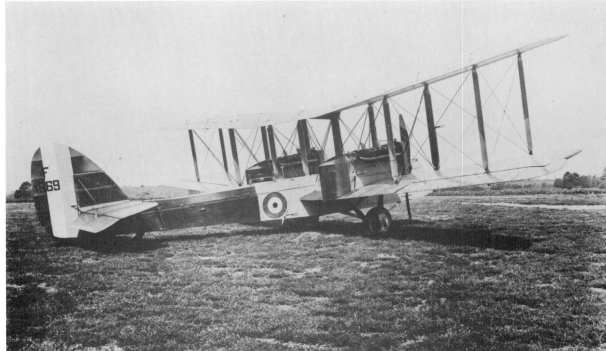

116

SQUADRON USE

No. 51 Sqn, Marham (first prototype only, for evaluation); No. 104 Sqn., Azelot (two D.H.10s only up to the Armistice). Post-

Armistice service with RAF Squadrons Nos. 60, 97, 120 and 216.

ance trials by the French *Section Technique de l'Aéronautique* at Villa-coublay on or before 25 September.

The D.H.10A variant was evidently considered acceptable, for it is probable that the aircraft ordered from Mann, Egerton & Co. Ltd. would have been completed as D.H.10As or 10Cs. In photograph **117**, F8423 is seen apparently in RAF hands. The extent to which D.H.10As might have been used by squadrons can only be conjectured. The RAF's forward Programme of

Development to 1 June 1919 foreshadowed two D.H.10 squadrons joining the Expeditionary Force, one in March and the other in April 1919; while in the Independent Force one D.H.9 squadron would be re-equipped with D.H.10s in November 1918 and one new D.H.10 Squadron (No. 121) would come in December, another (No. 122) in January 1919, two more in February and three in March, thus giving the Independent Force a total of eight D.H.10 squadrons by March 1919. Additionally, it

was intended to re-equip one D.H.6 anti-submarine squadron with D.H.10s in April 1919 and a further two in May. Had the war and production continued, at least some of these new units would surely have received some D.H.10As. Under Air Ministry Order No. 688 of 1 September 1921 the D.H.10 was declared to be the standard type, whereupon the D.H.10A, 10B and 10C became obsolete.

It would appear that the threat to the supply of Liberty engines that led

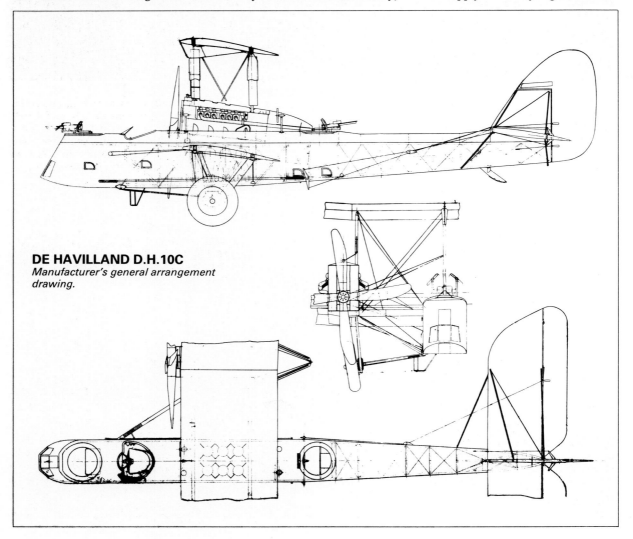

DE HAVILLAND D.H.10C
Manufacturer's general arrangement drawing.

117

to the reversionary installation of a
Rolls-Royce Eagle VIII in the
D.H.9A B7664 (see photograph 96)
caused similar engine changes to be
provided for in D.H.10s and 10As.
The designation D.H.10B existed in
respect of a variant with Eagle VIII
engines, presumably a D.H.10 in
which Eagles replaced the Libertys;
and it is certain that the D.H.10C was
a D.H.10A in which that substitution
had been made. No D.H.10B has yet
been positively identified, but E5557
(seen in photograph 118) and F8441
are known to have been D.H.10Cs.
The former, built by Airco, was
operated commercially in 1919 by
Aircraft Transport & Travel Ltd.

118

DE HAVILLAND D.H.11 OXFORD

Role: Three-seat bomber.
Powerplant: 2 × 320hp ABC Dragonfly.
Armament: Two 0.303in Lewis machine guns, both on Scarff ring mountings, one on bow cockpit, the other on dorsal cockpit; bomb load of about 1,000lb.
First flight: January 1920.

The D.H.11 (photograph **119**) was apparently conceived in June 1918 not only to meet official requirements for a long-range fighter-reconnaissance type but also to meet those for short-range and long-range day bombers. By 7 August 1918 its mock-up had been inspected and detail design work was in hand; two weeks later the fuselage was being erected. The name 'Oxford' was officially bestowed on the type very early in September 1918, but work was suspended in mid-month 'pending development of the Dragonfly engine' and to let the firm concentrate on other experimental types. By mid-November it was decided that, in common with several other types designed for the infamous ABC Dragonfly engine, two high-compression Siddeley Pumas would be fitted to the first Oxford, with the distinction Mark II. This, of course, never came about, though modifications were in hand in December 1918. By 31 January 1919 the aircraft was fully erected, its wings were being covered, and the intention then was to fit Dragonfly engines as originally planned. Although it had been intended to order three prototypes, only one, H5891, was built (Contract No. 35a/2150/C.2485, Aircraft Manufacturing Co.). Apparently it did some flying in 1920, but its Dragonfly engines doomed it to extinction and the development designated D.H.12 was never built.

119

DE HAVILLAND D.H.14 OKAPI

Role: Two-seat bomber.
Powerplant: 1 × 600hp Rolls-Royce Condor.
Armament: One fixed 0.303in Vickers machine gun synchronized by Constantinesco CC gear; two 0.303in Lewis machine guns on Scarff ring mounting on rear cockpit; six 112lb bombs or equivalent.
First flight: Late September 1920.

The type number D.H.13 was not used. The D.H.14 would have been a potent bomber if the war had lasted longer. It was very much a 'stretched' D.H.9A, designed to have the new Rolls-Royce Condor engine. An order for three prototypes had been recommended before 2 October 1918; two weeks later it was reported that Galloway Atlantic engines would be fitted, as Condors would not be available. By 30 October the wood and metal com-

RAE

120

121

delivered as military aircraft, J1938 and J1939, both had Condor engines but obviously had to wait until these were ready. J1938 was completed by 29 September 1920, and underwent leisurely evaluation at the RAE and Martlesham until it crashed and was burnt out at Burnham Beeches on 10 February 1922. Photograph **120** was taken at Farnborough. The second D.H.14, J1939, was completed late in 1920 and went to Martlesham in the spring of 1921; photograph **121** was taken there. In November 1921 it was fitted with a Condor Ia engine, but the aircraft was written off in April 1922 after being damaged beyond repair. A third aircraft built under Contract No. 35a/3365/C.3909, J1940, was completed as a D.H.14A, G-EAPY.

ponents of the fuselage and wings of the first aircraft were finished and ready for assembly; and by the end of January 1919 the fuselage and tail unit were complete and the wings were being constructed. On 2 October 1918

it was recorded that the name 'Okapi' had been allocated to the type – and that its makers had notified their adoption of the name 'Airco' in place of 'Aircraft' as their trade name. In the event, the two D.H.14s that were

DE HAVILLAND D.H.15 GAZELLE

Role: Two-seat bomber-reconnaissance aircraft.
Powerplant: 1 × 500hp Galloway Atlantic.
Armament: One fixed 0.303in Vickers machine gun synchronized by Constantinesco CC gear; one 0.303in Lewis machine gun on Scarff ring mounting on rear cockpit; bomb load of 660lb.
First flight: July 1919.

Despite its type number, D.H.15, this aircraft preceded the D.H.14 by some months. Its official name, 'Gazelle', had been allocated by 4 September 1918, at which date it was recommended that an order be given for one aircraft. Because it was simply a D.H.9A fitted with a 500hp Galloway Atlantic in place of the standard Liberty, early progress was rapid. By

18 September the airframe was ready for the engine and radiator. Deliveries of Atlantic engines had begun in July 1918, and by the end of the year 72 had been delivered of the 200 ordered. Nevertheless, the sole D.H.14, J1937 (Contract No. 35a/3015/C.3446), was not completed until July 1919; the aircraft is seen in photograph **122**. It went to Martle-

sham in May 1920, but by then any need for it had gone and it was not developed further. The RAF's Programme of Development to 1 June 1919 expected the D.H.15 to replace the D.H.4 in one squadron of the Independent Force in January 1919 and envisaged that squadrons equipped with the type would join the Independent Force in March/May 1919.

122

APPENDICES

APPENDIX A: AIRCRAFT SPECIFICATIONS

Type	No. (date) of trial report	Engine(s)	Aircraft serial number	Condition/ bomb load	Type of propeller	Dimensions, ft:ins			Wing area (ft²)
						Span	Length	Height	
D.H.1	–	80hp Renault	–	–	Integrale, Dwg. no. 69	41:0	29:11⅝	10:11½	362.25
D.H.1A	CFS 225 (18/19)	120hp Austro-Daimler[1]	4605	–	Integrale,	41:0	28:11¼	11:2	362.25
D.H.2	CFS (18 Oct. 1916)	100hp Gnome Monosoupape	–	Petrol capacity 26.3 gal.	Integrale, Dwg. no. 70	28:3	25:2½	9:6½	249
	–	110hp Le Rhône 9J	–	Petrol capacity 33 gal.	Integrale, Dwg. no. 70	28:3	25:2½	9:6½	249
	–	110hp Le Clerget 9Z	–	–	–	–	–	–	–
D.H.3	CFS M.36 (2 and 9 Jul. 1916)	2 × 120hp Austro-Daimler	–	–	–	60:10	36:10	14:6	793
D.H.3A	–	–	7744	–	–	–	–	–	–
D.H.4	M.64 (Sep. 1916)	200hp B.H.P. No. 1/W.D.7820	–	Prototype;	Dwg. no. 2328	42:4⅝	30:8	10:1	434
	M.64A (Sep. 1916)	200hp B.H.P. No. 1/W.D.7820	–	Prototype; 262lb bomb load	Dwg. no. 2328	42:4⅝	30:8	10:1	434
	M.152A (Nov. 1917)	230hp Galloway Adriatic No. 5094/W.D.22768	A7671	No bomb load	A.M.1329	42:4⅝	30:8	10:1	434
	m.152A (NOv. 1917)	230hp Galloway Adriatic No. 5094/W.D.22768	A7671	4 × 112lb bombs	A.B.7037	42:5⅝	30:8	10:1	434
	M.145 (Sep. 1917)	230hp Siddeley Puma No. S.D.5028/W.D.22702	B9458	No bomb load	A.M.1329	42:4⅝	30:8	10:1	434
	M.145B (Oct. 1917)	230hp Siddeley Puma No. S.D.5028/W.D.22702	B9458	2 × 112lb bombs under wings	A.B.703	42:4⅝	30:8	10:1	434
	M.145C (Nov. 1917)	230hp Siddeley Puma No. S.D.5028/W.D.22702	B9458	2 × 112lb bombs under wings, 2 × 112lb under fuselage	A.B.703	42:4⅝	30:8	10:1	434
	M.83 (Mar. 1917)	250hp Rolls-Royce Mk III (Eagle III) No. W.D.10071	A2129	Early production D.H.4; no bomb load	–	42:4⅝	30:8	10:5	434
	M.136 (Aug. 1917)	375hp Rolls-Royce Eagle VIII	A7446	No bomb load	D.G.2610	42:4⅝	–	11:0	434
	M.258 (July 1919)	353hp Rolls-Royce Experimental G	A7819	No bomb load	A.B.9150	42:4⅝	30:8	10:1	434
	M.92 (April 1917)	230hp R.A.F. 3a No. W.D.6583	A2168	No bomb load	D.G.2442	42:4⅝	29:8	10:5	434
	–	400hp Sunbeam Matabele	A8083	–	–	42:4⅝	–	–	434
	M.116 (July 1917)	260hp Fiat A-12 No. Fiat A/12841	A7532	No bomb load	D.G.2213	42:4⅝	29:8	10:5	434
	M.116A (July 1917)	260hp Fiat A-12 No. Fiat A/12841	A7532	2 × 230lb bombs	D.G.2213	42:4⅝	29:8	10:5	434
	–	400hp Liberty 12	–	–	–	42:5¾	29:7	10:9	429.5
	French report	300hp Renault	–	No bomb load	Chauviere	42:4⅝	–	–	434
D.H.5	M.76 (9 Dec. 1916)	110hp Le Rhône 9J	A5172	Prototype	–	25:8	21:0	8:8	224
	M.117 (July 1917)	110hp Le Rhône 9J No. 9107/8007, W.D.10609	A9186	–	L.P.1708	25:8	22:0	9:1½	212.1
D.H.6	–	90hp R.A.F. 1a	–	–	–	35:11⅛	27:3½	10:9½	436.3
	N.M.239 (12 Nov. 1918)	90hp Curtiss OX-5	B2903	Without flotation gear	A.D.543	35:11⅛	–	–	414
	N.M.239 (12 Nov. 1918)	90hp Curtiss OX-5	B2929	With flotation gear and 130lb 'bomb' load	A.D.543	35:11⅛	–	–	414

[1]Otherwise referred to as a Beardmore engine.

Weight (lb)		Maximum speed (mph) at altitude (ft)							Climb to (ft) in mins:secs					Ceiling (ft)		Endurance (hr)
Empty	Loaded	GL	3,500	5,000	6,000	6,500	10,000	15,000	3,500	5,000	6,500	10,000	15,000	Service	Absolute	
1,356	2,044	–	80	–	–	–	–	–	11:15	–	–	–	–	–	–	–
1,610	2,340	90	–	90	90	–	86	–	–	10:25	–	27:30	–	13,500	–	–
943	1.441	93	–	90	90	86	77	–	–	8:25	–	24:45	–	14,000	–	2¾
1,004	1,547	92	–	85	–	–	–	–	–	–	–	31:00	–	–	–	3
–	–	–	–	–	–	–	–	–	–	–	–	–	–	–	–	–
3,980	5,810	95:1	–	–	–	–	87	–	16:12	23:30	58:00	–	–	8,500	–	8
–	–	–	–	–	–	–	–	–	–	–	–	–	–	–	–	–
2,010	2,945	–	–	–	–	117	113	105	–	6:30	9:30	16:20	29:00	–	–	4½
2,010	3,148	–	–	–	–	112	109	103	–	8:05	11:00	19:00	–	–	–	4½
2,209	3,267	–	–	–	–	–	110	100.5	–	–	9:30	16:55	34:55	17,000	–	–
2,209	3,641	–	–	–	–	–	104.5	–	–	–	13:10	24:55	–	13,500	–	–
2,197	3,234	–	–	–	–	–	114	106.5	–	–	11:00	18:55	–	17,500	20,000	4½
2,197	3,386	–	–	–	–	–	109.5	101	–	7:48	10:30	19:12	21:12	16,000	–	–
2,197	3,610	–	–	–	–	–	106	–	–	11:48	15:30	–	–	13,500	–	–
2,303	3,313	–	–	–	–	117	113	102.5	–	–	8:55	16:25	36:40	16,000	18,000	3½
2,403	3,472	–	–	–	–	136.5	133.5	126	–	–	5:12	9:00	16:30	22,000	23,500	3¾
2,468	3,526	–	–	–	–	–	118	110	–	–	7:30	12:55	23:35	18,500	–	–
2,304	3,304	–	–	–	–	120	117.5	110.5	–	–	8:00	14:15	29:20	17,500	19,500	4
–	–	–	–	–	–	–	122	110.5	–	–	–	8:35	16:00	21,000	22,600	–
2,306	3,360	–	–	–	–	114	111	103	–	–	8:35	£5:35	32:55	17,000	19,000	4½
2,306	3,822	–	–	–	–	110	106.5	–	–	–	–	26:40	–	14,000	14,500	–
2,391	3,582	124.7	–	–	–	120	117	113	–	–	–	14:00	–	–	19,500	3
–	–	–	–	–	–	At 2000m 120.5	At 3000m 115.6	At 4000m 109	To 1000m 3:35	–	To 2000m 7:45	To 3000m 12:50	To 4000m 19:50	–	–	–
1,006	1,486	–	–	108	–	104	100	–	–	5:42	8:25	16:18	–	14,000	–	–
1,010	1,492	–	–	–	–	–	102	89	–	–	6:55	12:25	27:30	16,000	–	–
1,460	2,027	–	–	–	–	66	–	–	–	–	29:00	–	–	–	–	2¾
1,539	1,926	–	73	–	–	–	–	–	–	20:30	–	–	–	–	8,250	–
1,624	2,141	–	68	–	–	–	–	–	–	25:00	–	–	–	–	5,000	–

Type	No. (date) of trial report	Engine(s)	Aircraft serial number	Condition/ bomb load	Type of propeller	Dimensions, ft:ins			Wing area (ft²)
						Span	Length	Height	
D.H.9	M.146D (Nov. 1917)	230hp Galloway Adriatic No. 11/W.D.15434	A7559	Prototype; no bomb load	A.M.1329	42:4⅝	30:6	11:2	434
	M.146E (Nov. 1917)	230hp Siddeley Puma	A7559	Prototype; no bomb load	A.M.2627	42:4⅝	30:6	11:2	434
	M.156A (Nov. 1917)	230hp Siddeley Puma No. 5019/W.D.22693	C6051	2 × 230lb bombs	A.M.2627	42:4⅝	30:6	11:2	434
	M.156B (Dec. 1917)	230hp Siddeley Puma No. 5019/W.D.22693	C6051	3 × 112lb bombs and cut-out in lower wing	A.M.2627	42:4⅝	30:6	11:2	434
	M.205A (Nov. 1918)	290hp Siddeley Puma (high compression)	D5625	No bomb load	A.B.7931	42:4⅝	30:6	11:2	434
	M.205A (Nov. 1918)	290hp Siddeley Puma (high compression)	D5625	2 × 112lb bombs	A.B.7931	42:4⅝	30:6	11:2	434
	M.171A (Feb. 1918)	260hp Fiat A-12	C6052	No bomb load	A.M.2627	42:4⅝	30:6	11:2	434
	M.247 (Nov. 1918)	430hp Napier Lion	C6078	No bomb load	A.M.5012	42:4⅝	30:9½	11:7¾	434
D.H.9A	M.182 (Mar. 1918)	375hp Rolls-Royce Eagle VIII	C6350	No bomb load	A.M.2610	45:11⅜	30:3	11:2	486.73
	M.182 (Mar. 1918)	375hp Rolls-Royce Eagle VIII	C6350	2 × 230lb bombs	A.M.2610	45:11⅜	30:3	11:2	486.73
	M.182 (Mar. 1918)	375hp Rolls-Royce Eagle VIII	C6350	2 × 230lb and 14 × 20lb bombs	A.M.2610	45:11⅜	30:3	11:2	486.73
	M.227 (Sep. 1918)	375hp Rolls-Royce Eagle VIII	B7664	2 × 230lb bombs	A.M.2610	45:11⅜	30	10:10	486.73
	M.213 (July 1918)	400hp Liberty 12 No. 17616. A.62050	C6122	No bomb load	A.B.22699	45:11⅜	29:10	11:4	486.73
	M.213A (Aug. 1918)	400hp Liberty 12 No. 17616. A.62050	C6122	2 × 230lb bombs	A.B.22699	45:11⅜	29:10	11:4	486.73
USD-9A	Wilbur Wright Field (4 Oct. 1918)	400hp Liberty 12	–	No bomb load	X-6305	46:0⅛	30:2⅞	10:6	490
	Wilbur Wright Field	400hp Liberty 12	–	450lb bomb load	X-6305	46:0⅛	30:2⅞	10:6	490
D.H.10 Amiens Mk I	M.194A (April 1918)	2 × 230hp Siddeley Puma 5897-A23571 & 5248-A22922	C8658	As Home Defence aircraft with crew of 2	A.M.2628	62:9	38:10⅛	14:6½	787
	M.194A (April 1918)	2 × 230hp Siddeley Puma 5897-A23571 5248-A22922	C8658	As day bomber with crew of 2	A.M.2628	62:9	38:10⅛	14:6½	787
Amiens Mk II	–	2 × 360hp Rolls-Royce Eagle VIII	C8659	–	–	62:9	38:10⅛	14:6	834.8
Amiens Mk III	M.217 (July 1918)	2 × 396hp Liberty 12	C8660	Light bomb load	A.M.5019	62:11	39:6	14:7	833.5
	M.217 (July 1918)	2 × 396hp Liberty 12	C8660	Heavy bomb load	A.M.5019	62:11	39:6	14:7	833.5
	M.221 (Aug. 1918)	2 × 405hp (high compression) Liberty 12	C4283	Light bomb load	A.M.5019	65:6	39:7⁷⁄₁₆	14:6	837.4
	M.221 (Aug. 1918)	2 E 405hp (high compression) Liberty 12	C4283	Heavy bomb load	A.M.5019	65:6	39:7⁷⁄₁₆	14:6	837
D.H.10A Amiens Mk IIIA	M.225A (Sep. 1918)	2 × 405hp (high compression) Liberty 12, Nos. 18233/823/62140 and 18253/829/62143	F1869	Light bomb load	X3012	65:6	39:7³⁄₁₆	14:6	837.4
	M.225A (Sep. 1918)	2 × 405hp (high compression) Liberty 12, Nos. 18233/823/62140 and 18253/829/62143	F1869	Heavy bomb load	X3012	65:6	39:7⁷⁄₁₆	14:6	837.4
D.H.11 Oxford	–	3 × 320hp A.B.C. Dragonfly	H5891	–	I.P.C.5053	60:2	45:2¾	13:6	719
D.H.14 Okapi	–	600hp Rolls-Royce Condor	–	–	–	50:5	33:11½	14:00	617
D.H.15 Gazelle	–	500hp Galloway Atlantic	J1937	–	–	45:11⅜	29:11	11:4	486.73

Weight (lb)		Maximum speed (mph) at altitude (ft)							Climb to (ft) in mins:secs					Ceiling (ft)		Endurance (hr)
Empty	Loaded	GL	3,500	5,000	6,000	6,500	10,000	15,000	3,500	5,000	6,500	10,000	15,000	Service	Absolute	
2,193	3,283	–	–	–	–	116	110.5	102	–	–	11:05	19:55	42:25	16,000	18,500	4½
–	3,280	–	–	–	–	–	114	106	–	–	8:40	15:20	30:05	18,000	–	–
2,203	3,669	–	–	–	–	–	111.5	97.5	–	–	11:00	20:05	45:00	15,500	17,500	4½
2,203	3,585	–	–	–	–	–	104.5	95.5	–	–	12:30	23:20	62:00	14,000	–	–
2,232	3,327	–	–	–	–	–	116	106	–	–	7:50	13:55	28:00	17,500	–	–
2,232	3,503	–	–	–	–	–	114	103	–	–	9:30	16:35	34:25	17,000	–	–
2,460	3,600	–	–	–	–	–	117.5	107.5	–	–	9:00	16:00	32:20	17,500		–
2,602	3,725	–	–	–	–	–	140	135	–	–	4:55	8:10	14:35	24,000	–	–
2,705	3,800	–	–	–	–	–	125.5	116	–	–	7:00	12:10	22:55	20,000	22,000	4½
2,705	4,223	–	–	–	–	–	118	104.5	–	–	8:40	15:35	33:40	16,000	–	–
2,705	4,815	–	–	–	–	–	110.5	–	–	–	11:00	20:35	–	14,000	–	3½
2,832	4,733	–	–	–	–	–	115.5	107.5	–	–	10:00	17:50	36:35	17,000	–	6
2,770	4,220	–	–	–	–	–	120	114	–	–	6:50	11:50	22:50	19,000	21,000	5¾
2,800	4,645	–	–	–	–	–	114.5	106	–	–	8:55	15:50	33:00	16,500	–	5¾
2,815	4,322	126.2	–	–	–	121.2	117.6	109.5	–	–	7:30	13:15	26:15	18,700	20,000	3½
2,815	4,872	121.5	–	–	–	118.5	115.5	95.5	–	–	11:40	19:30	49:0	14,400	15,000	–
5.004	5,814	–	–	–	–	–	–	–	–	–	8:40	15:10	29:50	18,000	–	–
5,004	6,950	–	–	–	–	–	100.5	89.5	–	–	11:25	20:55	50:30	15,000	–	3½
–	8,500	117.5	–	–	–	–	–	–	–	–	–	–	–	–	–	–
5,600	8,500	–	–	–	–	–	113.5	105	–	–	9:20	16:35	35:20	16,000	–	4
5,600	9,000	–	–	–	–	–	–	–	–	–	10:05	18:30	–	15,000	–	–
5,585	8,500	124	–	118.5	–	117.5	115	110	–	6:00	8:10	14:35	29:55	17,500	–	6
5,585	9,000	–	–	118	–	116.5	112.5	106	–	6:30	9:00	16:05	34:20	16,400	–	5¾
5,750	8,500	131	–	130	–	128	124	117	–	4:45	6:25	11:00	20:30	19,000	20,000	6
5,750	9,000	–	–	–	–	126	121	112	–	–	7:05	12:25	24:30	17,500	–	5¾
3,795	7,000	–	–	–	–	(est.) 117	(est.) 115	–	–	–	–	(est.) 13:30	–	–	–	3¼
4,484	7,074	–	–	–	–	–	122	–	–	–	–	–	–	–	–	–
2,312	4,773	139	–	–	–	136.5	133	–	–	–	4:55	8:12	–	–	20,000	–

APPENDIX B: AIRCRAFT CONSTRUCTION AND FINISH

CONSTRUCTION

All wartime de Havilland aircraft were essentially of wooden construction. In all but the D.H.1, D.H.2 and D.H.5, the forward half of the fuselage was covered with plywood, as was the rear end of the fuselage; radiator cowlings and over-engine deckings were of aluminium. All other covering was of fabric. Conventional wire cross-bracing was fitted in the fabric-covered rear portion of the main fuselage girder; in the forward portion, rigidity and true form were provided by diagonal wooden members and the plywood covering. In the D.H.5 fuselage similar principles were applied, but the plywood-braced (and extensively fretted) portions were concealed within the built-up fairings, and the whole was fabric-covered from firewall to sternpost (but at the Royal Aircraft Factory A9403 was experimentally given a full plywood covering on its fuselage). Flight surfaces were of wooden construction with fabric covering; some trailing edges were formed of streamline-section steel tubing.

FINISH

In general, upper and side areas of all types were finished in P.C.10 dark khaki; undersurfaces were left as clear-doped natural fabric. As several of the illustrations show, some D.H.1s, 2s, the D.H.3, and some of the earliest D.H.4s had clear-doped natural fabric areas.

PRESERVED EXAMPLES (OF WARTIME TYPES)

D.H.6:   C9449 (parts only), South African Air Force Museum, Pretoria.

D.H.9:   F1258 in Musée de l'Air et de l'Espace, Le Bourget; F1287 (G-EAQM) in Australian War Memorial, Canberra; IS-8 in South African National Museum of Military History, Saxonwold, Johannesburg.

D.H.9A: F1010 in Royal Air Force Museum, Hendon.

APPENDIX C: PRODUCTION CONTRACTORS

The Aircraft Manufacturing Co. Ltd. Hendon, London N.W.	All types	National Aircraft Factory No. 1 (Managed by Holland, Hannen & Cubitt Ltd.) Waddon, Surrey	D.H.9
The Alliance Aeroplane Co. Ltd. (Waring & Gillow Ltd.), Cambridge Road, Hammersmith, London W.14	D.H.9, D.H.10	National Aircraft Factory No. 2 (Managed by Crossley Motors Ltd.) Heaton Chapel, Stockport	D.H.9, D.H.10
F. W. Berwick & Co. Ltd. Park Royal, London N.W.10	D.H.4, D.H.9, D.H.9A	Palladium Autocars Ltd. Felsham Road, Putney, London S.W.15	D.H.4
The Birmingham Carriage Co. Birmingham	D.H.10	Ransomes, Sims & Jefferies Ipswich	D.H.6
The British Caudron Co. Ltd. Broadway, Cricklewood, London N.W.2	D.H.5	Savages Ltd. King's Lynn, Norfolk	D.H.1, D.H.6
Canadian Aeroplanes Ltd. Strachan Avenue, Toronto, Ontario	D.H.6	Short Brothers Rochester, Kent	D.H.9
Cubitt Ltd (properly Holland, Hannen & Cubitt)	(See National Aircraft Factory No. 1)	The Siddeley-Deasy Motor Car Co. Ltd. Park Side, Coventry	D.H.10
The Daimler Co. Ltd. Coventry	D.H.10	The Vulcan Motor & Engineering Co. (1906) Ltd. Crossens, Southport, Lancashire	D.H.4, D.H.9, D.H.9A
The Darracq Motor Engineering Co. Ltd. Townmead Road, Fulham, London S.W.6	D.H.5	Waring & Gillow Ltd. (Alliance Aeroplane Co. Ltd.) Cambridge Road, Hammersmith, London W.14	D.H.4, D.H.9
The Glendower Aircraft Co. Ltd. 54 Sussex Place, South Kensington, London S.W.3	D.H.4	G. & J. Weir Ltd. Cathcart, Glasgow	D.H.9
The Gloucestershire Aircraft Co. Ltd. Cheltenham, Gloucestershire	D.H.6	Wells Aviation Co. Ltd. 30 Whitehead Grove, Chelsea, London S.W.8 (Sub-contractors to Waring & Gillow)	D.H.9
The Grahame-White Aviation Co. Ltd. Hendon, London N.W.	D.H.6		
Harland & Wolff Ltd. Belfast	D.H.6	Westland Aircraft Works Yeovil, Somerset	D.H.4, D.H.9, D.H.9A
The Kingsbury Aviation Co. Kingsbury, London N.W.	D.H.6	Whitehead Aircraft Co. Ltd. Old Drill Hall, Townshend Road, Richmond	D.H.9, D.H.9A
Mann, Egerton & Co. Ltd. Aircraft Works, Norwich	D.H.9, D.H.9A, D.H.10		
Marsh, Jones & Cribb Ltd. Leeds	D.H.5		
Morgan & Co. Leighton Buzzard	D.H.6		